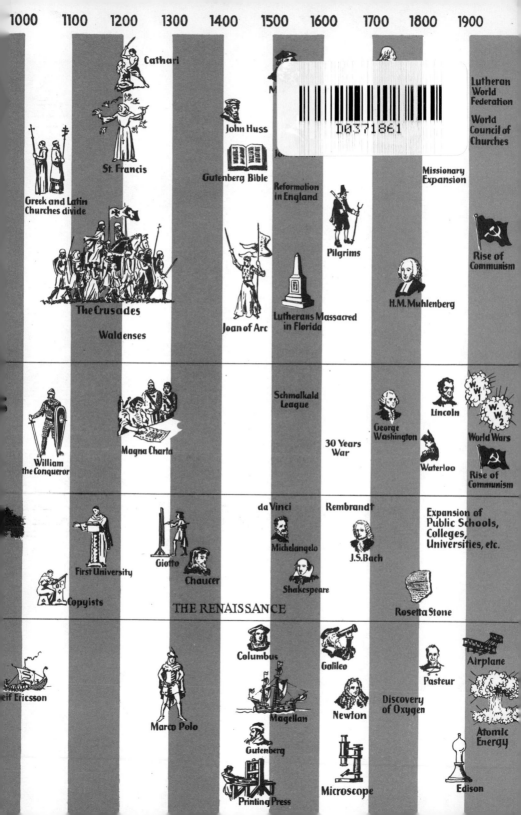

1000 1100 1200 1300 1400 1500 1600 1700 1800 1900

Cathari

John Huss

Gutenberg Bible

St. Francis

Greek and Latin Churches divide

Reformation in England

Lutheran World Federation

World Council of Churches

Missionary Expansion

The Crusades

Pilgrims

H.M.Muhlenberg

Rise of Communism

Waldenses

Joan of Arc

Lutherans Massacred in Florida

William the Conqueror

Magna Charta

Schmalkald League

30 Years War

George Washington

Lincoln

W.W.1

W.W.2

World Wars

Waterloo

Rise of Communism

da Vinci

Rembrandt

Expansion of Public Schools, Colleges, Universities, etc.

Michelangelo

J.S.Bach

First University

Giotto

Chaucer

Shakespeare

Copyists

THE RENAISSANCE

Rosetta Stone

Columbus

Galileo

Airplane

Pasteur

Leif Ericsson

Marco Polo

Magellan

Newton

Discovery of Oxygen

Atomic Energy

Gutenberg

Microscope

Edison

Printing Press

LUTHER and the
REFORMATION

by **REGINALD W. DEITZ**

W. KENT GILBERT, *Editor*

CONCORDIA COLLEGE LIBRARY
2811 N. E. HOLMAN ST.
PORTLAND, OREGON 97211

Illustrated by **PAUL REMMEY**

JOHN GEISZEL, *Maps and Charts*

THE WEEKDAY CHURCH SCHOOL SERIES • GRADE VIII

MUHLENBERG PRESS • PHILADELPHIA

Lu Th.
BR
308
D325

Copyright, 1953, by
The Muhlenberg Press
Philadelphia, Pennsylvania

Seventh Printing

P.O. 4198

The Biblical quotations are from *The Holy Bible, Revised Standard Version*, copyright by the Division of Christian Education of the National Council of Churches of Christ in the United States of America, and are used by permission.

2266

Printed in U. S. A.

UE1427

Foreword

Around the turn of the sixteenth century there was an old German schoolmaster who used to doff his cap every morning to his pupils, so the story goes, not because of what the boys were but out of respect for the men they might become. Certainly the old schoolmaster could never have dreamed how right he was. For among the boys seated before him was a lad who would one day awake a world.

Within the pages of this book you will read the story of that awakening, for this is the story of Martin Luther and the Reformation which he began. It is the tale of one of the most exciting periods in the history of man.

Within these pages you will read how the Christian church grew from a feeble handful of men to become the greatest power in the greatest empire on earth. You will see how this giant of a church grew sick with the abuses of its own power and began to die from within. Then a new, clear note was sounded when a lone monk challenged the evil around him. What happened as a result of that challenge changed the course of history for the next four centuries and is still changing it today. This will be the story you read.

Luther and the Reformation is the eighth grade course in the *Weekday Church School Series.* This study book is to be used with the teacher's guide. Together they form the complete course of study.

Permission to use the following quoted material copyrighted by other publishers, is hereby acknowledged with appreciation.

Bainton, *Church of Our Father,* Charles Scribner's Sons, 1941, quotation on page 10, line 31.

P. Smith, *Life and Letters of Martin Luther,* Houghton Co., copyrighted by Mrs. Priscilla Robertson, 1914, quotations on page 75, line 34; p. 95, l. 22; p. 96, l. 32; p. 97, l. 11; p. 99, l. 5 and 33.

1-26-66 Clark C²

24083

Flick, *Rise of the Medieval Church*, G. P. Putnam's Sons, 1909, quotation on page 13, line 11.

Flick, *Decline of the Medieval Church*, Alfred A. Knopf, Inc., 1930, quotation on page 27, line 13.

Bettenson, *Documents of the Christian Church*, Oxford University Press, Inc., 1944, quotation on page 16, lines 8 and 13.

Schweibert, *Luther and His Times*, Concordia Publishing House, 1950, quotations on page 33, line 8; p. 42, 1. 18; p. 59, 1. 26; p. 69, 1. 1; p. 81, 1. 24; p. 82, 1. 8.

Bainton, *Here I Stand*, Abingdon-Cokesbury Press, 1950, quotations on page 36, line 24; p. 40, 1. 6; p. 44, 1. 22; p. 47, 1. 27; p. 50, 1. 7; p. 56, 1. 21; p. 60, 1. 12; p. 61, 1. 6; p. 62, 1. 16; and 34; p. 65, 1. 4 and 14; p. 67, 1. 19; p. 68, 1. 15; p. 70, 1. 25 and 27; p. 71, 1. 4; p. 74, 1. 33; p. 89, 1. 11; p. 94, 1. 29, 31, and 34; p. 95, 1. 16, 17, and 20.

Lucas, *Renaissance and Reformation*, Harper and Bros., 1934, quotation on page 27, line 26.

Sweet, *Story of Religion in America*, Harper and Bros., 1939, quotation on page 136, line 25.

McNeill, *Makers of Christianity*, by Henry Holt and Co., 1935, permission requested, quotations on page 14, line 10; p. 15, 1. 17.

P. Smith, *Age of the Reformation*, Henry Holt and Co., 1920, permission requested, quotations on page 18, lines 2 and 5; p. 30, 1. 13; p. 106, 1. 26; p. 109, 1. 21.

Coulton, *Medieval Panorama*, Cambridge University Press, 1947, quotations on page 20, lines 16 and 34.

Chart on page 130 is reproduced with the permission of the National Council of Churches of Christ in the United States of America.

The Editor

Contents

I

On the Way to Power

1. Church and State

This story begins long ago in a troubled age when bishops were kings and kings were bishops. At least that's the way many felt and that's how they fought. The real issue was power and authority. That struggle burst into flame when a simple monk named Martin Luther stood before the emperor himself and said there was a power greater than either bishops or kings. But that was in the sixteenth century. Let's go back to the beginning of our story.

There was a time when Christians had been content to be without power at all—except the power of love. The Romans for a long while had not known what to do with Christians in their empire. That they were wicked, dangerous, unpatriotic seemed quite certain. Unfriendly critics snooping around a place of Christian worship heard phrases about eating "my body" and drinking "my blood" and decided that here surely was a band of cannibals. More intelligent folk thought that to worship a crucified criminal was a disgusting superstition. (Remember Paul had said that the cross was "to the Greeks foolishness"! *I Corinthians 1:23*)

Most people agreed that Christians were unsocial when they refused to attend the vulgar shows of the theatres and the bloody public games where men's lives were sacrificed to entertain the crowd. Almost all agreed they were unpatriotic because they refused to take part in the rite which symbolized the Roman empire—worship of the Roman emperor. To Christians this was idolatry.° When they insisted there was only one Lord, Jesus Christ, the emperors resolved to "break" them, to stamp them out.

A number of Roman rulers from Nero on tried their hand at persecution. The first empire-wide oppression was ordered by the Emperor Decius in A.D. 250. For years Christians of all walks of life lived under the threat of death. And thousands

---

° Look up words marked with an asterisk in the list of difficult words on page 151.

did pay with their lives for their loyalty to Jesus Christ. Often they were brought into the arena and burned or attacked by wild animals—all for the amusement of the mob. But all this was to change in a surprisingly short time.

Early in the fourth century a rising young general of the Roman armies saw that instead of being dangerous, Christians might actually be the strongest, most reliable, best-organized group in the empire. So General **Constantine** hitched his star to that of the Christian God. And presently when he seized control of the empire, he granted first tolerance and then special favors to the Christians. The time was 313. In less than three centuries Christianity had risen from nothing to become the official religion of the mighty Roman empire.

Constantine was first of all a politician. His empire had one head, one citizenship for all free men, one law. In addition it now had one religion. This last, he felt was important. So when trouble broke out in the Christian church—disagreements about policy, belief, practice—he stepped in as emperor. Having granted special favors to the church, he did not care to let things get out of hand. For example, churchmen had been arguing bitterly about whether Jesus Christ was really God's Son. When the first great, church-wide council met at Nicea in Asia Minor in 325 to see what could be done about the fuss, who should be there seated among all the bishops and priests and taking part in the discussions but the Emperor himself— even though he had never even been baptized. Repeatedly Constantine took a hand in the internal matters of the church; so did his sons and later successors. Some church leaders sensed what was happening. One of them walked up to Constantine's son one day and said,

"If you are going to persecute me, I will bear it rather than deny the truth, but remember that God has given to you the Empire and to us the Church. If we steal the government we oppose God, and if you meddle with the Church you do wrong."

An important part of the story of Western Europe for more than a thousand years centers about this issue—the relation of church and state. Actually Christianity and government can

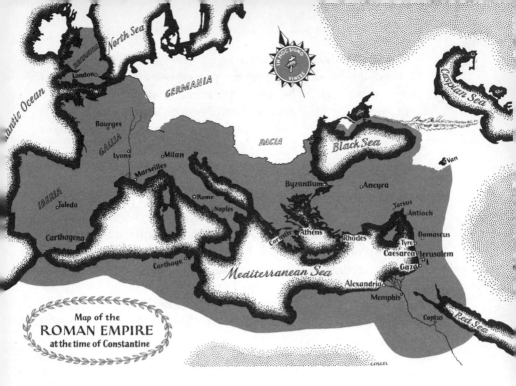

Map of the
ROMAN EMPIRE
at the time of Constantine

never be completely separated from each other. So princes meddled in the church, and bishops stole the government—when they could. Their successes and failures, their plans and intrigues were bound some day to set the stage for the Reformation, but not until both church and empire had grown sick with evil.

2. In the Dark Ages

In spite of the work of able rulers like Constantine, the Roman Empire was on the down-grade. Slowly it decayed at the center and fell apart at the edges. Administration faltered. Old customs failed. Business became poor. Population declined. Uncouth barbarian tribes invaded and settled down in ancient civilized countrysides. The civilization which had existed so brilliantly around the Mediterranean for more than a thousand years was clearly sick and dying.

Later historians have called the centuries which followed "the Dark Ages." They were long years of chaos, disorder, turmoil, war, stagnation. Yet beneath the turbulent scene a bright new civilization seemed to be taking shape in Europe.

Meanwhile the old struggle for power between bishops and princes continued. The chief difference was that now one bishop spoke for all the church in Western Europe. Throughout Christendom he was known as the *pope* (which means "father").

In the early centuries of the medieval period (the Middle Ages) the church became so involved in secular affairs that it almost lost its spiritual character. Many bishops were feudal princes who lived in luxury, violence, and wickedness. Their offices were bought and sold. Church appointments were almost completely controlled by kings and emperors.

In the eleventh century a group of high-minded reformers appeared in the church. The best way, they felt, to lift the church from its terrible disgrace was to make the pope truly powerful, supreme in the church. The leader of this movement was Hildebrand who in 1073 became **Pope Gregory VII.** He went even further. He dared to claim that the pope as God's representative on earth was supreme not only in the church but in worldly affairs and over kings as well.

3. Pope and King

On an April day in 1073 Hildebrand was conducting a special service in St. John Lateran Church in Rome in memory of the pope who had just died. For twenty-five years he had been the power behind the papal throne, and yet he was unprepared for the cry which suddenly burst forth from the crowd, "Hildebrand, Hildebrand shall be our pope. St. Peter chooses our Archdeacon Hildebrand!" One of the cardinals came forward and made a little speech. Protesting and in tears Hildebrand was hurried off to the throne of St. Peter where they put upon him the scarlet robe and tiara (crown) of the pope. He took the name Gregory VII.

Gregory believed that the pope was God's representative on earth and therefore the lord of all the world. Clergy and laymen* alike were completely subject to his will. The popes before Gregory had not even been able to rule the church. He claimed the right to rule not only in the church but also over all earthly authorities. Throughout the church conditions began to improve as Hildebrand's stern measures for reform were announced. Yet there was much resistance.

In 1075 at a council in Rome Gregory had a rule passed making it unlawful for any church office to be received from or given by a layman—for example, a prince. Henry IV, emperor of Germany, regarded this as a violation of his royal rights and defiantly appointed the bishop at Milan. Gregory threatened the king with excommunication;° Henry insulted the pope's messengers. Gregory was presiding at a council in Rome when a royal herald burst in. "My lord, the king, and the bishops of the Empire," he announced in an insulting tone, "do by my mouth command you, Hildebrand, without delay to resign the Chair of Peter, for it is unlawful for you to aspire to so lofty a place without the royal consent."

Gregory and his supporters were of course indignant. Henry was excommunicated. This meant he could receive none of the sacraments° of the church; all others were forbidden to assist him in any way; his subjects were freed from obeying him and a curse was laid on Germany.

Suddenly Henry discovered that his followers were not as loyal as he thought. Enemies used the opportunity to attack him. His position was getting worse; he was slipping. His only hope was to make peace with the church.

Meanwhile Gregory had started for Germany where he planned to complete Henry's overthrow and humiliation. Henry was anxious to forestall this at all costs. So in the dead of winter he made his way through the Mt. Cenis pass of the Alps into northern Italy. Gregory had reached the castle at Canossa. There on January 25, 1077 Henry appeared outside the gates seeking admission to the pope's presence. For three days he stood barefoot in the snow, clad in sackcloth and fasting from morn to night. Friends urged the pope to be merciful, but Gregory probably suspected Henry's insincerity and realized that he had been robbed of a victory in Germany. Yet a humble penitent could not be ignored. Henry was forgiven and restored to communion on his promise of complete obedience.

Gregory was a man of small stature but his flashing eyes be-

trayed a restless, driving spirit. Friends called him "Holy Satan!" By sheer force of spiritual weapons he had compelled the most powerful ruler of Europe to beg forgiveness. Here was a great, if temporary, landmark in the struggle for power. For the moment the bishop of Rome was supreme.

Actually Henry had stooped to conquer. Shrewdly he rebuilt his power in Germany. A few years later he marched into Italy and after a long siege conquered Rome and drove out his old enemy. In May 1085 Gregory died in exile at Salerno. His last words were bitter, "I have loved justice and hated iniquity; therefore I die in exile."

Yet Hildebrand had not failed. With a single purpose in mind, he had staked out claims for the papal office which have

14

never been surrendered. At times his successors have been able to make his sweeping dreams of absolute power over all human affairs come true. Of no one was this more true than of Lothario Conti, Pope Innocent III.

4. Bright Sun at High Noon

When **Innocent III** was elected pope on January 8, 1198, he was only 37 years old and not even a priest. Nevertheless he had been a recognized leader of the College of Cardinals* for almost ten years. He was a churchman of distinguished background, superior education, and outstanding ability. His ideal was the same as Hildebrand's: to make the Roman pope the supreme ruler, temporal* as well as spiritual.

Before he had even been crowned he declared that, just as the light of the moon is borrowed from the sun, so the King who rules men's bodies borrows all his power from the pope who rules men's souls. In his coronation sermon Innocent said, "I am he whom the Lord hath placed over His household; yet who am I that I should sit on high above kings and above all princes?"

This was precisely the position which Innocent realized. Within a few years he made himself unquestionably both political and spiritual head of Europe. If a century or two before the church had been helpless before the greed of princes and the evils of its own servants, now it was supreme. Innocent corrected many wrongs within the church including the corruptness in the papal household. He was a superb politician who, in the name of God and largely with spiritual weapons, dominated the life of his age. He reformed the church, persecuted heretics, and made kings toe the mark. Besides influence, diplomacy, and money (the pope was the wealthiest power in Europe), his weapons were excommunication and interdict.

Excommunication made a person a social outcast. His property could be seized. He could not receive any of the sacraments of the church. If he did not repent, death and hell were his sure doom. In the case of a king, his subjects were freed from obedience to him. An interdict was directed against a city or kingdom. When it was imposed, almost all religious ceremonies and sacraments were suspended, and even the civil government practically came to a halt. Since the Roman church was believed to be the supreme spiritual authority, excommunication and interdict were very effective.

The authority which Gregory had claimed and Innocent had used was eventually explained in a statement issued almost a century later by **Boniface VIII.** In 1302 Boniface solemnly declared, "There is one Holy Catholic and Apostolic Church, and outside this Church there is neither salvation nor remission of sins."

He declared bluntly that both political and spiritual authority are in the power of the church. The poorest priest is superior to the noblest king. He concluded, "We declare, state, define and pronounce that it is altogether necessary to salvation for every human creature to be subject to the Roman pontiff."

Thus the church controlled both men's consciences and their daily lives. The church was a thoroughly-organized, highly-centralized state. In the struggle for power between pope and kings there was no question for the moment as to who was on top.

5. The Perils of Power

A great English historian, Lord Acton, once said, "Power corrupts, and absolute power corrupts absolutely." He could very well have had in mind the Christian church or at least the popes of the Middle Ages. At any rate the church, which had struggled to win complete authority in order to save men's souls, presently lost its own soul and began to decline.

Part of the difficulty grew out of the fact that the church could not decide whether to be an out-and-out political state or a great spiritual community. It tried to be both, but the two positions did not mix well. There were many high-minded and honest popes concerned about man's spiritual welfare. But even they were distracted from the church's main task and burdened by all their duties as politicians and statesmen. Unfortunately there were many popes who had little or no concern about spiritual matters. Under them the official church almost forgot the Christian gospel and its Lord.

A Diet met in the city of Augsburg, Germany, in the spring of 1518. (A "diet" was a gathering of representatives of the many German cities, states, and principalities.) The pope had sent a representative to ask that a tax be levied on the clergy (priests, bishops, etc.) and the wealthier nobility. He needed money to fight the Turks who were invading Europe. The request was refused in violent language, and the Diet declared that the real enemy of Christianity was not the Turk but "the hound of hell" in Rome! What had happened to make men feel like that about "the vicar of Christ on earth"?

One reason was that people resented the vast claims to power and authority made by the pope. Everyone admitted the pope's spiritual supremacy. But the new nations of Europe did not like to have him meddling in politics. The kings of Europe were growing stronger in their own countries. They were in no mood to give in to the tyranny of the pope.

In the second place people everywhere in Europe were horrified by the greed of the pope and the court (or *curia*) which surrounded him. On the basis of actual records it has been shown that the annual income of the papal court was not less than $1,100,000—this in a day when the total income of the king of France (or France's national government) was less than half that amount. This money came from taxes laid upon clergy and people throughout Christendom. The popes had a corps of agents who traveled about seeing that the money came in.

In addition it became common practice to sell hundreds and hundreds of positions at the papal court plus many of the higher offices throughout the church. The price would usually run about eight or ten times the expected income. When some of the later popes needed money, they created new offices and sold them. These "expectations" provided a kind of gambling system. Men bought a place in line for appointment to offices not yet vacant. Sometimes up to ten expectancies were sold for a single position!

As a result of this greed almost anything the church had to offer was available for cash. If a man had the patience and money to work through the papal court, he could get almost any sin forgiven, any kind of conduct approved. Said one high papal official, "The Lord desires not the death of a sinner but that he should pay and live." The system, of course, offered little to the poor.

No wonder **Pius II** (d. 1464) had to confess, "If we send ambassadors to ask aid of the princes, they are mocked; if we impose a tithe on the clergy, appeal is made to a future council; if we publish an indulgence and invite contributions in return for spiritual favors, we are charged with greed. People think all is done merely for the sake of extorting money. No one trusts us. We have no more credit than a bankrupt merchant."

What had happened was that the popes forgot they were the heads of a church. Their worldliness alarmed and repelled earnest Christians everywhere. For example, **Alexander VI's** (1492-1503) chief sin as pope was to enrich his children. Crimes and scandals abounded. He lived a purely secular* life spending his time in hunting, dancing, stage plays, and indecent orgies. Under him the church reached its lowest level of degradation.

Julius II (1503-13) did little for the church but was a great patron of the arts. Some of the greatest works of painters like Raphael and Michaelangelo were commissioned by him. St. Peter's Cathedral was started during his office.

Julius' successor was **Leo X** (1513-21), a play-boy who had been made a priest at six, a cardinal at 13, and was now elected pope at 38. Life to him was just one long carnival. He spent money recklessly, entertained wildly. He said, "Let us enjoy the papacy, since God has given it to us."

Not all the popes were as bad as these, but few of them had a real sense of spiritual mission and their responsibility as head of the church. No wonder thousands of men and women were bitter about the church's demands and resented its authority. Times were ripe for a change.

6. Like Pope, Like Priest

It would be incredible if corruption and decay at the head of the church had not appeared also at the other end of the ladder. In 1502 the foremost scholar of Europe, Erasmus, said that lay people disliked priests so thoroughly that to call a man a "cleric," or a "priest," or a "monk" was an insult. We should not suppose that there were no good priests or honorable bishops in the church. Yet the number who disgraced their high offices was so large as to be tragic.

One of the first charges made against ministers in this period was that they were immoral. Too often they were throughly unworthy. Many were given to drink, some kept taverns and gambling houses, were lazy, greedy, gluttonous. They were guilty of improper relations with women, of trading, embezzling, forgery, neglecting parish property (leaky roofs, broken fences), selling the sacraments. Priests who could afford it went in for gaudy dress, jewels, and high living like the secular princes. They entertained lavishly, had many servants and large stables. Frequently those who were drunk at night read mass in the morning and then spent the day in the public-house or out hunting. The amount of this sort of thing was shocking. Scores of records have come down to the present which suggest that these vices were, if anything, more common among the clergy than among the laity.

Whenever medieval writers discussed their priests, they were sure to mention not only their immorality but also their igno-

rance. There were hundreds of instances of priests who did not know enough Latin to be able to understand the service of the Mass even though Latin was the church's official language. About the time of the Reformation, Bishop Hooper in England found scores of clergy who could not name the author of the Lord's Prayer or tell where it was to be found. Dean Colet complained that the church swarmed with "a multitude of unlearned and evil priests."

Conditions in the parishes were made even worse by two evils that many complained of but no one did anything about —*pluralism* and *absenteeism*. It was possible for a priest to get himself appointed to several positions at the same time. This often took a bit of bribing, perhaps even some contacts at Rome, but it was done. For example a dispensation° from Rome in the late 13th century gave Boniface, son of Thomas, the right "to hold two benefices with cure of souls (i.e. parishes) without being obliged to be ordained or to reside." In other words the young man was given permission to receive the income from two parishes without living in or doing the work of either—in fact without even being a priest!

A survey by the bishop in the county of Oxford, England in 1520 showed that fifty-eight out of 193 parishes had absentee priests. If a man were conscientious, he paid a less fortunate priest a small sum to live in his parish and do the work. If he were not conscientious, he forgot the matter. The vicars who filled in for the priests were forced to live as a rule on starvation wages. They were frequently a poor, shiftless lot who squeezed the people to get more money.

One duty the priest could not escape — that of collecting taxes. A ten per cent tax was imposed for the church upon every parishioner. In addition there were many other demands which added up to a considerable burden. When men were unwilling to pay—as they often were—the priest was required to "curse them by the authority of the Court of Rome, within and without, sleeping or walking, going and sitting, standing and riding," and so forth through twelve lines of print that ended with a condemnation to hell. Many a good priest himself poorly paid and knowing the problems of the poor, did all he could to avoid excommunicating° those who lapsed in their payments.

Meanwhile multitudes of priests neglected their true ministry—saying Mass, hearing confession, administering the other sacraments, serving the sick, helping the poor. Worship was often a noisy routine in which there was little of devotion or piety. Christianity had become institutionalized, commercialized, secularized. Many priests were minor officials, not men of God. They were the local agents of a system that traded in religion, grabbed for money, and gave little in return. Men feared the priest as the representative of divine justice. Some they loved as servants of the Lord. Many they hated for their greed, corruption, and worldliness, for making piety a counterfeit, the salvation of souls a business, and eternal life a means to tyranny.

7. Like Priest, Like People

With such leadership in the official church, it is no wonder that Christianity, as understood and practiced by the average believer, was at many points ignorant, corrupt, and superstitious. The Christian's outlook was largely pessimistic and dark. Life here and now was a mighty struggle between good and evil. There was little in this world but greed, violence, war, hunger, pain, disease, suffering, death. Pious souls longed to escape. This life was but a preparation for the better life in the hereafter. Wise men lived religiously in the hope that, when death came, they might gain happiness in heaven. To make sure of this, thousands of men and women forsook the world and entered monasteries where they could prepare themselves quietly for heaven.

Medieval men believed the world was evil in part because of evil spirits who could be controlled by magic and were used by witches for their wicked purposes. Witches, it was thought, were agents of the devil. They held meetings to which they flew on broomsticks and where they worshiped the devil with disgusting rites. Witches could cause hail, make crops fail, turn healthy children into invalids.

Churchmen fought this superstition vigorously, but they

had little to say about another—the worship of the saints and the veneration of relics. Admiration for the heroes of the Christian life was embroidered with legend and supersition. For many people the saints had become special deities and popular Christianity, a religion of many gods. Like pagans worshiping their idols, merchants prayed for a rich haul, gamblers for luck. Men prayed to St. Apollonia for relief from toothache, to St. Agatha to prevent earthquakes, to St. Clarus for cure of eye-trouble, and to St. Lupus for protection against wolves.

Collecting and selling relics of the saints, of Christ, and of the Apostles became a big business. Most of them, of course, were frauds, but thousands of items were shown throughout Europe. Many were supposed to have magical powers. Erasmus remarked that there seemed to be enough pieces of wood of the true cross to build a ship. Cologne displayed the bones of the Three Wise Men. The shroud that covered Christ's body was shown at Turin. At Wittenberg people could look at a part of the burning bush which Moses saw!

Of all the saints, the Virgin Mary was the most popular. Since people more and more tended to think of Jesus as a righteous judge, Mary, the queen of heaven, was called upon to intercede° on behalf of helpless sinners. They thought of her as a great wonder-worker and called on her to save them in all kinds of difficulties.

Religious experience centered upon the sacraments, especially penance (with confession) and the mass. In penance a man confessed his sins to the priest. If he were truly sorry, he could be assured of God's forgiveness. As an evidence of his genuine repentance, certain penalties or penances were imposed: a pilgrimage, perhaps, or some humble service. Long before the Reformation a system of substituting money payments for these penalities had developed. The pardons were called indulgences and were supposed to be relaxations of the church's punishment for sin. In the popular mind, however, the indulgence was thought to purchase God's forgiveness as well.

By the thirteenth century, the church made another interesting and, as it turned out, popular discovery. It found that it had for disposal a surplus of merit accumulated by the saints and by our Lord. The extra supply of merit could be parcelled out by the church to help those who were not able to get enough for themselves. The power of the priest lay in his strategic position; he was the only one who could put sinners in touch with the means of salvation.

Greatest of all miracles was that of the mass—which only the priest could perform. The medieval church taught that at a certain point in the service of the Lord's Supper, the bread, though it appear still to be bread, is really Christ's body, and the wine, though it have all the qualities of wine, is actually Christ's blood. So at every mass Christ comes in his physical presence, and his sacrifice on Calvary is repeated all over again to save the faithful.

There were other sacraments, too: baptism, confirmation, marriage, ordination (consecrating a man to be a priest), and last rites (when a person is dying).

And so as the machinery of the church became more and more complicated and the people were caught helplessly in the grinding of its wheels, a wave of unrest began to sweep through Europe. Soon that wave was to become a torrent.

II

Voices of Faith

So far, this account has dwelt upon the false, the ignorant, the wrong, the worldly in the life of the Roman Catholic Church in the days before the Reformation. This is necessary if we are to understand the awesome torrent which broke loose when one monk spoke. In vast areas of its life the church had lost its soul.

However, we should not exaggerate these evils so much as to forget that in spite of all the rottenness and corruption there were multitudes of devout and sincere believers. And there were hundreds of pious priests amid the prevailing evil who had a sense of spiritual mission and sought to serve both Jesus Christ and his children. The leaders of the Reformation, when it finally came, were themselves products of that church. Along with the evil, there was good. We must look at some of the groups and men who lifted up their voices within the church to protest the wrongs and, if possible, work a renewal of life.

8. Heretics

Some who criticized or tried to reform the church were known as heretics, that is, people who reject the church's teachings. Throughout this period there were many heretics but two groups in particular caused the church a lot of trouble.

One was called the Albigenses or **Cathari** ("purists"). Perhaps disappointed crusaders returning from the Holy Land picked up ideas which had been floating around in the East for a long time and had caused difficulty in the ancient church. Many became convinced that the world is evil, the body bad. Therefore people should get rid of the world and the body as far as possible, in other words, be "pure." They refused to fight, objected to marriage, did not believe in churches. Many of their beliefs were strange and fantastic; their views were certainly not Christian. People followed them, however, because they criticized the corruptions of the church severely and in contrast led peaceable, moral lives.

The Cathari were spread all over southern Europe and were especially strong in southern France. Efforts to convert them were not very successful. Finally in alarm the pope (Innocent III, see page 15) proclaimed a crusade. The fine countryside was laid waste, towns were destroyed, and thousands of people slaughtered. The strength of the Cathari movement was broken.

The **Waldenses**, like the Cathari, were branded as heretics though they never used such fantastic teachings. They were the followers of a merchant of Lyons named Peter Waldo who, though uneducated, learned large portions of the Bible in French and decided to take its teachings very literally. He gave away his money and began to preach. He made the Bible the sole law for his life. His followers went about in twos, wore simple woolen robes and sandals. Forbidden by the church to preach, they would not keep silent and became increasingly critical of some of its practices. Eventually they were called heretics and persecuted. It was their ignorant and, it was felt, improper use of the Bible that led the church in 1229 to forbid laymen to possess the Scriptures—especially in any other translation than the official Latin.

To deal with heretics, the popes after Innocent III appointed some officials called inquisitors. They were to hunt out those who held false beliefs and turn them over to the government for punishment—burning at the stake. The "inquisition," as it was called, proceeded secretly; a man might not even know the names of his accusers. Sometimes he would be tortured to make him confess. If convicted, his property could be seized. Eventually terrible devices like the rack (for stretching a man's body) and screw (for squeezing his fingers) were used to make men tell "the truth"! These unchristian methods were excused on the grounds—as Innocent III suggested—that heresy is treason against God. It was felt that if heretics went unpunished, God would punish the whole world. It was better for a few to die than for all to suffer, better for a man's body to burn on earth than for his soul to be lost and burn forever in hell. This strange view of Christianity dominated the church for years and brought terror to the hearts of thousands.

9. Reformers and Rebels

Torture may make men afraid but seldom does it change their opinions. In medieval Europe the evils in the church were so great that many men cried out in protest. Some became boldly defiant of the church's teachings and ran the risk of being denounced and burned for heresy.

One who had followed this dangerous path in England was **John Wyclif**, a lean and pious scholar who later became a priest. He was most concerned about the ignorance and superstition of ordinary people. To combat this he made a translation of the Bible. It was an important and careful piece of work. Because printing had not yet been invented, however, the translation could not be circulated widely. Wyclif's followers were called **Lollards.** Many of them he trained as "poor priests" to go out and preach to the people from the Bible. Perhaps largely because there was a little more freedom in England than elsewhere, Wyclif escaped serious persecution. He died in 1384. In 1428 his body was dug up and burned to show he had been a heretic. His ashes were thrown into the river, but his ideas had already escaped to Europe.

At the University of Prague, Wyclif's ideas deeply impressed an eloquent young preacher from the country, named **John Huss.** Soon he, too, was denouncing the wealth and corruption of the clergy and saying things which did not agree with the official teaching of the church. Because such a large number of the clergy were German, Huss's attacks sounded to many like the voice of Bohemian patriotism. Presently Huss found himself the leader of a strong party.

This unrest and such stinging criticisms could not be tolerated very long. Huss was condemned as a heretic and excommunicated. He retreated for safety to southern Bohemia.

In 1414 a great church council assembled at Constance in Switzerland. The Emperor, many princes and civil authorities, more than two hundred bishops, and as many as three hundred professors were present. They came together to consider several problems in the life of the church. One was heresy.

Huss was invited to appear. The Emperor Sigismund gave him a sealed promise of safe conduct that no matter what might happen he would be sent home safely. Soon after Huss reached the city, however, he was thrown into prison. He spent more than six months in loathsome conditions, bound by chains, in pain from illness, and half-starved. When finally tried, he was accused of absurd beliefs which he had never expressed. He had many enemies in the assembly but few friends. He was called upon to deny his heresies, but the noble priest refused "to lie in the face of God." He was formally degraded at a ceremony in the great cathedral before all the nobles, doctors, churchmen, and the Emperor who blushed for shame when reminded of his promise. On his head they put a paper cap three feet high decorated with devils.

"We commit your soul to the devil," said the church judges.

"And I commit myself to the most gracious Lord Jesus," Huss quickly replied.

That afternoon they led him out to a nearby meadow. He was chained to the stake by his neck. Straw and wood were piled up to his chin, and the fire lighted. He sang, "Christ, thou Son of the living God, pity, pity thou me," until smoke and flames made him unconscious. His ashes were shoveled into a wheelbarrow and dumped into the river Rhine—so there would be no relics! The next day the cardinals, bishops, clergy—and the Emperor—held a solemn service of thanksgiving to God!

A critic of an entirely different sort was **Savonarola** of Italy. He was an educated and cultured man, but he became a monk because, as he told his father, of "the miserable condition of the world." So much "immorality, robbery, pride, idolatry, cursing" was there, he said, that "almost no one can be found who has any regard for what is good." Presently he was appointed preacher in Florence. He spared neither prince nor pope nor people. He denounced sins in high places and low. The Florentines fell under the spell of the preaching monk with the solemn face and glowing eyes. They set out to reform both themselves and their city.

Alexander VI (Rodrigo Borgia) one of the most worldly and immoral men to head the church, had become pope in 1492. He became alarmed at Savonarola's influence. With the help of the preacher's enemies within Florence, Savonarola was

CONCORDIA COLLEGE LIBRARY 27
2811 N. E. HOLMAN ST.
PORTLAND, OREGON 97211

MAP OF
SOUTHERN EUROPE
in the time preceding
LUTHER

John Wyclif 1384

Erasmus 1536

Thomas à Kempis 1380-1471

John H. 141

Peter Waldo 12th Century

The Cathari 13th Century

Savonarola 1495

Moors driven from Spain 1490-1500

Columbus 1492

finally condemned. In April 1498 he was arrested, tortured, and declared guilty of heresy. In May he was hanged and burned, the victim of politics in the church.

10. Critics

Not all who wished to reform the church went so far as to become heretics or run the risk of untimely death. Among the most important of these gentler critics were the **Mystics**. What disturbed them chiefly was the unspiritual kind of Christianity shown by the official church. Men were bargaining with God for their happiness when they should be hungering for his presence. They believed all that the church taught and worshiped devoutly, but they sought to escape from earthly concerns in a pure fellowship with the Eternal. Master Eckhart (d. 1327) was a philosopher; Henry Suso (d. 1366), a poet and romantic; John Ruysbroeck (d. 1381), a man of

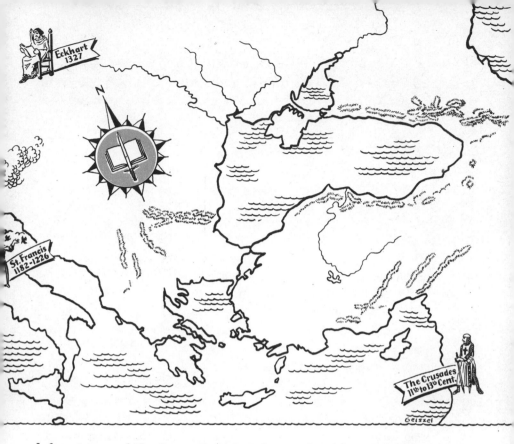

lofty visions of the love of God; John Tauler (d. 1361) was a fervent preacher and evangelist who said that pure religion is to be "drowned in God," "intoxicated with God," "melted in the fire of his love." Groups of humble people like "The Friends of God" and later "The Brethren of the Common Life" practiced the quiet life of earnest prayer, devotion, searching for God, and serving one's fellows. They did not say much about the evils in the church, but their lives rebuked the worldly and kept fresh a vast spring of pure spirituality. Thomas a Kempis, author of the classic *The Imitation of Christ,* was one of them.

Different in temper were the **Humanists,** who were not so much interested in making the church religious as reasonable. They were the scholars of the new age, devoted to the study and printing of the writings of the ancient church fathers and of the Bible. The leading humanist of the day, and perhaps the leading figure of his generation, was **Erasmus** (d. 1536).

29

He retold the Bible stories in simple language everyone could understand. He made fun of the superstition and magic of popular Christianity. He wanted to get rid of the arguments of the theologians and make of Christianity a simple, moral way of life. He often referred to "the philosophy of Christ."

Erasmus did not storm and rage at the evils of his day. He did not use a battering ram but a fine, sharp sword. With keen wit he insinuated and undermined—and hoped to reform the church. In one of his books a young man is asked what he has done for Christ. The youth related how he gave a drubbing to a stupid Franciscan monk for his criticisms of Erasmus' New Testament. He pounded his face to jelly and with the book "gave him three resounding whacks on the head in the name of the Father and of the Son and of the Holy Ghost."

"What do you think of that?" concluded the young man.

"That," replies the friend, "was truly evangelic; defending the gospel by the gospel. But really it is time you were turning from a brute beast into a man."

On another occasion when a priest at Strassburg Cathedral was showing him around and became boastful of the noble background of all who were admitted to office there, Erasmus remarked quietly that he was indeed honored to be in company so noble even Jesus could not have met its requirements!

Erasmus and his humanist colleagues—like John Reuchlin, John Colet, Sir Thomas More, and many others—were high-minded, cultured gentlemen. They were devoted to both scholarship and moderation. They hoped to win the intelligent allegiance of men by declaring the simple truth and gradually to destroy the ignorance and superstitution of the old church. They hoped also to lift up the church from its fallen ways by a gentle insistence upon goodness and sharp scorn for corruption. They could not see that the evil in the church was so deep-rooted that it would take more than ridicule, telling wit, and earnest scholarship to change its ways. They were men of moderation, tolerance, good will. They had conviction but little passion. A man of different temper was needed to voice the longings of multitudes and to say again what had always been the church's true mission. Presently he appeared.

Finding the Gospel .

11. Schoolboy

When **Martin Luther** came to Erfurt as a university student
in the spring of 1501, it was the largest and richest city he had
ever seen. It lay in a lovely setting below the Thuringian hills.
Round about were woodlands, orchards, and rich fields. Within
its stout walls the city was a bustling center of business. Colorful traders from all over Europe filled the city for the annual
markets. More than a hundred church organizations of various
kinds were to be found in the city. Most impressive of them
all was the cathedral towering above all others. Often it was
the scene of brilliant church pageantry.

The streets of Erfurt were crooked, narrow, and dirty. As
in other medieval° towns, the burghers threw their garbage
right into the streets. Pigs, goats, and other livestock wan-
dered about at will. Since the streets were unpaved, unlighted,
and often ran along streams and canals, they were very dangerous after dark. University rules allowed the students to go
out at night only when they carried a lantern and then only for
special occasions.

One night early in 1505, however, Erfurt's dark streets were
lighted by the smoky glow of torches. The narrow walls rang
with the flourish of trumpets and the noisy shouts of the people.
The whole town was cheering a group of happy young men as
they rode by on horseback. The young men had just passed
their examinations and earlier in the day had been solemnly
made "Masters of the University."

Among the seventeen masters on that February evening was
Martin Luther. Four years of study had ended in success. Now
he was ready to begin law as his father had wanted. That
night the new masters entertained the faculty at supper.

Yet less than six months later Luther gave another supper—
this time for some of his friends. It was a jolly affair, but as the
guests were leaving Luther announced that he was leaving
the university and going at once into a monastery. The next

day he entered the Augustinian cloister* in Erfurt and became a monk.*

But why? That's what everyone wanted to know, not least of all, Martin's father. He was bitterly disappointed at this sudden end to his son's promising career.

Martin Luther had been a normal boy. Though born in Eisleben (November 10, 1483) he had spent his boyhood in Mansfeld where his father was a miner. At first Hans and Margaretta had had to work desperately hard to support themselves and their large family. Gradually, however, through hard work and thrift Hans had prospered a bit, was able to buy a mine and lease others. He was even selected for a position in the town government.

Like all parents in those days Hans and his wife expected their children to behave and obey. Discipline was swift and severe. Yet in their rather dull, uneducated way Hans and Margaretta loved their boy and expected great things of him. Hans sent Martin to school and dreamed that some day he would be a prosperous lawyer.

Luther loved school though what he had to study would seem terribly dull to us and must often have seemed so to him.

Latin was almost the whole course of study—Latin grammar, readings, composition, literature, Latin hymns, prayers, and the Latin Bible. Of course, all this was very useful, for Latin was the language of the church, law, diplomacy, international relations, scholarship, culture. But most teachers did little to get beyond memorization.

In the normal course of things all schoolboys got whipped (as one regulation put it) "in the place that God has naturally provided." Misbehavior, poor work, or using German got one's name on the "wolf list," and at the end of the week there was a whipping for each mark. One day, Luther recalled, he was flogged fifteen times. That must have been a bad week! Then there was the wooden donkey mask which a boy caught speaking German had to wear until he caught somebody else. And so the boys were made to study by fear and shame.

Luther became an excellent student. In his teens his father sent him to school at Magdeburg (one year) and then at lovely Eisenach. He learned and grew and developed. He sat under a fine teacher named Trebonius at Eisenach.

Erfurt had seemed at first like a splendid, if sometimes wicked city. While there were temptations and opportunities for getting into trouble, a student's life was closely regulated at every point by the rules of the university. Luther lived in the Georgenburse or dormitory where he was under the close and careful watch of its Master. Because artificial light was so poor, students were expected to go to bed at 8 P.M. and get up at 4 A.M. Bells announced the schedule. The students had to wear special dress for every occasion. At meals parts of the Bible were read aloud.

Life, of course, had its lighter side and Luther at times must have been a rollicking companion. He was in love with life and the lovely German countryside. Luther had his friends, and he would often sing and play the lute for them.

12. The Religion of Fear

Then suddenly—the monastery.* Or was it so sudden? Martin's friends and family had no inkling of what was about to take place. But it is now quite clear that things were happening in the spirit of this young man that sometimes made him dreadfully afraid.

The simple fact is that Luther grew up in an age that was very religious and yet terribly uncertain about the most important religious questions. Martin's home life was rough, superstitious, and devout. Hans's mines and woods and home were, he believed, inhabited by elves, gnomes, witches, and spirits. Always the other world and the next life were close at hand. In every town, there were reminders of the way to heaven—steeples, spires, monasteries, priests, tolling bells, roadside shrines, monks, solemn processions, and praying pilgrims holding high their crucifixes while chanting songs. Everything about a boy's education was designed to build wthin him a deep respect for the church and a fear of God.

As a matter of fact, fear and hope alternated in medieval religious experience in such a way as to leave any serious person in doubt. Hell was described in horrible terms to frighten men into seeking God. Terrible fiends snatched at the soul of the dying. Christ was not only merciful redeemer but also terrible judge who condemned the wicked to the eternal fires of hell. Yet to help the penitent° from giving up hope, there was purgatory.° This was a place of temporary suffering before one was finally admitted to heaven. But how long was the time spent in purgatory? The church never said.

Of course, the church had suggestions to help the pious make his place in heaven secure. Sacraments, pilgrimages, indulgences, the prayers of the saints—all these could help. Relics were popular, and the church had at its disposal an abundance of merits to help the sinner. Most effective of all, however, was the life of the monk. To forsake the world and devote one's full time to prayer, confession, and good works—this, it was believed, was the surest way to make the gates of Paradise swing open when this brief life was over. Luther remembered seeing Prince William of Anhalt begging on the streets of Magdeburg and carrying a heavy sack on his back like a

donkey. "With my own eyes I saw him," he remembered years later. "He had so worn himself down by fasting and vigil that he looked like a dead man, sheer skin and bone, so that he died soon after. No one could look upon him without feeling ashamed of his own life."

The altar piece of Magdeburg showed a ship on its way to heaven. In it were only monks and priests while laymen struggled and drowned in the sea—except the few who caught the ropes thrown out to save them. And so one could assure escape from everlasting suffering by turning one's back on the world and crushing the flesh.

It was a somber, terrifying, and dangerous world in which men had to work out their salvation. Perils and uncertainties beset the average Christian at every turn. A man did what he

could but never could know that he had done enough. Only monkish self-denial and piety offered a sound hope. This all men understood.

These were the religious views which Luther accepted. On them he had been nourished at home, in school, and through all his associations. This was the religious outlook of ordinary people in a very religious age. Actually there was nothing unusual about Luther's ideas except the intensity with which he held them. And yet because of this intensity Martin Luther became more and more disturbed about the state of his soul. Moods of dark despair would sweep across his spirit, and he would wonder in fright about his standing before the Judge of heaven and earth. Years later he observed, "Doubt makes a monk." He doubted that "in the world" he could ever do enough to save his soul. Perhaps he was more troubled than usual during the spring months of 1505.

In June that year he spent a week or two in Mansfeld visiting his parents. On July 2 on his way back to Erfurt he was overtaken in the country by a severe thunderstorm. A bolt of lightning struck nearby and threw him to the ground. This, as all medieval men knew, was the very wrath of God! In'a flash he seemed to see his fate as he stood before Christ the terrible judge. He cried out in terror to his father's saint, the patroness of miners, "St. Anne help me! I will become a monk." This he believed was the call of heaven and, though he later regretted his promise, it had to be obeyed. Luther became a monk in obedience to God. To him it seemed that the will of the Lord was clear.

13. The Ways of a Monk

So foreign is monasticism° to most American Protestants that it is difficult for us to appreciate the kind of life young Martin Luther had entered. After a few weeks of observation he was received into the brotherhood as a novice.° About a year later, having satisfied the brothers as to his worthiness, he took the vows of a monk to be obedient, poor, and unmarried.

At his reception as a novice he knelt before the prior (head of the monastery) in a solemn service and declared that he desired "God's grace and mercy." He was reminded of the hardships of the monastic life. He was given the long flowing robe of the monk. It was like a white house dress and a black mantle. Then his hair was clipped and the top of his head shaved to form the "tonsure" (regular mark of a monk).

His room was a little cell, seven by ten feet, furnished simply with a table, chair, and straw bed. It had one window and was unheated. Noise or conversation was forbidden. No one was allowed to laugh. Martin was taught to walk with downcast eyes, how to conduct himself at meals, when and before whom to kneel or throw himself on the ground, how to take part in the daily services. He was given his share of lowly tasks to teach humility. He learned to get along on just two meals a day and with only one on the hundred or more fast days. Every act of every hour was regulated. Prayers were held seven times a day, beginning with matins° about two in the morning. Day after day he read the Bible. He confessed his sins humbly to his superior at least once a week. So in an orderly round of prayer, song, quiet companionship, meditation, and self-denial he sought what the church taught was the surest way to salvation. The church as the ark of salvation, the splendor of its sacraments and ceremonies, the hourly call to prayer, and its pious devotions were all congenial to his spirit. From groups, such as the Brethren of the Common Life, a rich devotional spirit was working through sections of the church, and this deep concern may very well have touched his spirit.

Outwardly the next ten years of Martin Luther's life were not in the least eventful. As soon as he became a full-fledged monk, he was told to study for the priesthood. He was ordained in Erfurt in April, 1507 and a few weeks later said his first mass. Almost at once he was instructed by his superiors to begin advanced study. In 1511 Luther was sent to the new university at Wittenberg to fill one of the teaching positions. As lecturer on the Bible, Brother Martin began an intensive study of the Scriptures. Sometime during the next two years, as he came to grips with the Word of God, a revolution took place deep in his troubled spirit. A light broke through the darkness of doubt. The change was not seen at once. The real results did not appear for years. In that moment of insight, however, a new age was born.

14. Dread of the Almighty

It is difficult for a young person today to appreciate what went on within Martin Luther during these years. We are interested in "fun," in a good time. This is an important part of even our religious activities. We do not dream of fearing God. We may approach him with a certain amount of reverence but never with dread. We are sure of his friendship.

Things were quite different with Martin Luther. Like millions of others in his day he was deeply concerned about his relation with God. Salvation was not a fact to be easily taken for granted but a goal to be pursued eagerly, hopefully, tremblingly. It was uncertainty about this all-important issue that had driven Martin Luther to become a monk. For a time, apparently, his uncertainty was satisfied. In following the monkish routine, his brethren told him, he was pursuing the sure path to heaven. For a while he was happy. Then suddenly his doubts began again.

One of the first signs of trouble came at the saying of his first mass in 1507. This event was something of a festive occa-

sion in a young man's life. Even Luther's father, who had been furiously angry when his son became a monk, appeared for the service. As it turned out, the elaborate ceremony gave the young priest a bad time. Any man was likely to face the ordeal with considerable dread, for the church taught that in this, the chief sacrament, the priest performs the miracle of transforming the bread and wine into the actual body and blood of Jesus Christ. It is this power which makes the priest superior to all other men, even kings.

Years later Luther recalled that when he came to the words in the service, "We offer unto thee, the living, the true, the eternal God," he was suddenly terror-stricken. How should a mere man address the mighty and eternal God? How could a sinner speak to majestic Holiness? Though he managed to stick it out, he almost fled from the altar. He finished limp and shaken.

Here was the heart of his problem. The absolutely holy God demands holiness in those who come before him. Luther, more honest than most of us, recognized his own sinfulness. He was *not* holy. How then could he be saved?

For such doubts the Roman church had some traditional answers. One was confession. When the priest whispered the words of forgiveness, all sins were supposed to be driven from the soul. Luther tried again and again and again through these years—and had to admit to himself that in bitter fact confession did not make him sinless.

The trouble was simply that Luther was more honest than most in recognizing the tricks of his own conscience. For sins to be forgiven they were supposed to be confessed. Yet after six hours of confessing, he could go out and think of sins he had forgotten. Even worse he realized that some sins a man cannot even recognize, still less remember. The trouble is deeper, he came to feel, than particular offenses which a man commits against God's law. Man's whole nature is corrupt, marred by sin, hostile to a holy God.

Another answer to Luther's doubts about salvation was supposed to be found in monasticism itself. This belief had led Luther to become a monk in the first place. Now he found that there were different degrees of piety within the monastery. So Luther resolved to do all the good works he could in order to win the asurance he sought. He fasted sometimes for three days in a row. He discarded blankets and almost froze to death in his cold cell. He drove himself with ceaseless prayers and vigils. "I was a good monk," he wrote later, "and I kept the rule of my order so strictly that I may say that if ever a monk got to heaven by his monkery it was I. . . . If I had kept on any longer, I should have killed myself with vigils, prayers, reading, and other work."

But the uncertainties were still there. Just when he would think he had done enough to be sure of God's favor, the doubt would come back, "But *have* you done enough?" He would drink in "the sweet praise and fine words" with which friends and superiors would praise his conduct. He would feel comfort in some beautiful and ancient hymn sung of an evening in the monastery church. Then suddenly he would come across a reference in the Bible to God's righteousness—and would be plunged into torment and despair. At times he felt wild hatred in his heart for this dreadful God who demands holiness of sinners and leaves them in an agony of uncertainty about their fate. "No tongue can tell, no pen can write," he says, "what a man suffers in such moments. . . . At such a time God in his wrath appears dreadful beyond all imagination. And like God, so the whole creation. No flight is possible. There is nothing that can comfort. Everything accuses."

15. Pilgrim to Rome

Luther's exhausting inner struggles and his quiet development as a scholar through these years were interrupted by one trip into the outer world. In the fall of 1510 he was sent to Rome by the brothers on business for the order. Altogether he was gone about six months. Rome in this day was a typical medieval city of about forty thousand. Ruins of its ancient glory were to be found everywhere—but now cows and goats grazed among the tumbled stones. There were a few impressive churches, but most of its artistic glories were yet to come.

During his stay in Rome Luther saw some old ruins, some

seventy monasteries, churches and hospitals, the palaces of the cardinals, and many other sites that must have seemed quite remarkable to a visitor from far off Germany.

However, Luther came to Rome not as tourist but as pilgrim. For this was the center of Christendom. No other place had so many sacred shrines, such precious relics, or the chance for such wonderful indulgences.* Rome had a single vault where forty popes and seventy-six thousand martyrs were buried. It was supposed to have a piece of Moses' burning bush, the napkin of St. Veronica, the chains of St. Paul, the leaning crucifix, a coin paid to Judas, eleven thorns from Christ's crown, a nail from the cross, some hair of the Virgin Mary, two pieces of the five loaves with which Jesus fed the multitude, the table used at the Last Supper, the rope with which Judas hanged himself! Thousands and thousands of years indulgence could be had by just looking at these objects.

In view of his wonderful opportunity (for he believed all these things were genuine) Luther was, as he said, "mad" with religious zeal and used his time in visiting and saying masses in order to pile up for himself and his relatives all the enormous spiritual benefits possible.

Yet the pious German monk was disillusioned. He was shocked by the silly gaiety, lack of reverence, unbelief, and immorality of Italian priests. Even more, the young monk was disturbed by doubts about whether his good works really were a way of salvation. Famous among the relics was the stairway of Pilate's palace up which Jesus was supposed to have been led. For climbing these on hands and knees and saying a prayer on each step it was possible, the church said, for the pilgrim to release some tormented soul from purgatory. Luther resolved to secure this benefit for his grandfather, Heine Luder. He even wished that his own parents were dead so that he could help them! Yet as he reached the top, the haunting doubt returned. "Who knows whether this is true!" he muttered to himself as he walked slowly away.

16. Light in the Darkness

Back at Wittenberg Luther was directed by his superior, Staupitz, to begin to study for his doctorate and the position of preacher and teacher. Staupitz tried to help Luther in his difficulties, but even he was baffled. "I don't understand it," he told Luther once. Only one thing is needed, he advised, that you love God. But how could a man love God, Luther asked in agony. How can a man love the angry, judging, damning God? How can you love the Christ who sends men into the flames of hell for eternity? Where, he asked, is the mercy and goodness of God? "I was . . . driven to the very abyss of despair," Luther sobbed, "so that I wished I had never been created. Love God? I hated him."

Not until April or May, 1513, did the light finally break through Luther's bleak misery. It happened quietly, suddenly, but very positively. He was preparing lectures on the Psalms when all his old troubles were roused by the word "righteousness" which he came across again and again. To understand it more thoroughly, he turned to *Romans* and read in *1:17*, "For in it (the gospel) the righteousness of God is revealed through faith for faith; as it is written, 'He who through faith is righteous shall live.'" Suddenly it dawned on him that there was an important grammatical distinction here. Luther reasoned this way—when the New Testament speaks of "the power of God," it is not talking about the power God possesses in himself but the power he implants in us. So, Luther went on, the righteousness of God is not the righteousness he possesses but the righteousness he gives to us. In other words, it is an act of forgiveness through which sinners are treated as though they were righteous. God is like a judge who suspends sentence and by personal, friendly interest wins back the criminal to a decent life. This is the doctrine of *justification by faith*. As Luther now discovered, it is the heart of the gospel message.

How does a man get right with God? What can a man do to be sure he is saved? Luther had a new answer now. It stayed with him to the end of his life. He had discovered a new God —no longer an angry, condemning judge but the God who sent his only Son to take upon himself the burden of our sin and to die at Calvary. On the cross is both God's terrible judgment upon our sin and his amazing love for us. And there is nothing we can do, nothing needs to be done, to win the love of God. We already have it. We must simply believe that he is like this, confess our sins truly, and receive his forgiveness. God is like the father of the prodigal in Jesus' story, who waits patiently for his wayward son to come home. And when we come, we do not have to bring a sackful of good works to bribe him into loving us. We have to come rather with that humble faith by which we trust God, and let him rule our lives.

This was the message which Luther discovered in the Bible. The teachers of the church, on whose works he had been trained, had strayed far from the path. They had erected a system of self-help which brought only doubt and misery to sincere, seeking souls. Now suddenly but very surely Luther began to discard this man-made system. Gradually a new idea of the Christian faith, based on the Bible, began to emerge. Luther had gone back to the gospel.

43

17. Changed Man

Luther's new discovery answered the doubts in his heart and filled his soul with peace. Otherwise it seemed for the time to make very little difference. Yet his new faith began soon to appear in his lectures and preaching. During these quiet years from 1513 to 1517 the young professor was thinking, writing, and feeling his way. In his lectures (on the *Psalms* and *Romans*) there is still much of the old scholastic° thought. This was Luther's heritage.° Yet within the old forms one can see the new idea of personal, spiritual Christianity emerging. His approach to the Bible had a freshness which contrasted sharply with the older interpretations. Students began to flock by the hundreds to hear this new teacher with the stirring message from the Word of God.

People not only listened to Luther; they believed him. He possessed the leader's natural ability to influence others. For example, a kind of *Who's Who* among German university professors, does not even mention Luther's name in 1514. Yet four years later he was not only the leading professor at Wittenberg, but also had won every other member of the faculty to his views.

Meanwhile he was busy. "I could use two secretaries," he wrote to a friend. It was difficult for him to find time for the daily devotions of a monk. In addition to his teaching he was regular preacher both in the monastery and in the parish church at Wittenberg. In 1512 he was put in charge of student-monks and in 1515 was made overseer of ten monasteries of the Augustinian order. Apparently his superiors had a high opinion of his ability.

Gradually Luther began to use his new understanding of the gospel as a standard for rating the church's teachings and practice. Criticisms and sharp comments appear in his lecture notes. Many of these complaints were probably never made public. They show that he was still a faithful son of the church but by no means a blind one. The conflict broke out, however, not when evils and abuses in the church reached a climax, but when, as a pastor, Luther saw the danger to human souls in one popular feature of the church's system.

IV
Fire in the Church

18. Purgatory and Punishment

To most medieval Christians purgatory° was more of a problem than hell. The Roman church taught that a sinner could escape hell by sincere repentance. But God's judgment was not all he had to worry about. The church had penalties, too. Originally these were very severe. Unless the sinner carried out these penances faithfully, he had to go through the pains of purgatory. Most people expected to spend some time there. Naturally they snatched eagerly at any way of shortening the stretch.

At first indulgences were just substitute penalities which the church permitted. For example, the sinner could make a pilgrimage or take part in a crusade in place of a seven-year fast on bread and water. But this system soon gave way to a worse one. The next step was to make it possible for men to *buy* an indulgence instead of *earn* one. If a man couldn't go on a crusade, he could gain the same benefits by giving the church the money it would have cost him to go. That did it! People who were afraid of purgatory (and who was not?) could now buy indulgences to shorten their future suffering. After awhile it was even possible to buy indulgences for friends and relatives already dead. As for the church, the popes played the game to the limit, for the sale of indulgences proved to be a fabulous money-maker. The "holy trade," as it was called, made the church the biggest financial institution in Europe.

Wittenberg, where Luther taught, knew plenty about indulgences. As a pious Catholic the **Elector Frederick** had amassed a remarkable collection of "genuine" relics. The pope had announced that people could win generous pardons by seeing these relics. The collection included a thorn from Jesus' crown, a piece of his swaddling clothes, a strand of his beard, a piece of gold brought by the Wise Men, a twig of Moses' burning bush. There were more than nineteen thousand holy bones. Pious folk who viewed these relics on All Saints' Day (November 1st) and made the required contributions received indulgences to reduce purgatory by 1,902,202 years, 270 days! The income supported the university and the castle church.

In the fall of 1517 a vigorous indulgence-seller named **John Tetzel** came peddling his wares not far from Wittenberg. Frederick would not permit him in Electoral Saxony because he had his own business to protect. Yet Tetzel was near enough that Wittenbergers could skip over and buy a "plenary" (complete) indulgence. **Pope Leo** had issued it to pay for the building of St. Peter's Cathedral. He promised forgiveness of all sins and freedom from all pains of purgatory.

There was more to this indulgence than met the pious eye. Albert of Brandenburg, though bishop of both Halberstadt and Magdeburg (and too young at that), wanted also to be made archbishop of Mainz. This, of course, was entirely against the church law. But he was sure money would talk—especially with Pope Leo. A bargain was struck. The great Fugger banking house of Germany advanced ten thousand ducats for Albert. Then, to help Albert pay off his debt, the pope issued the indulgence, the income to be split with him fifty-fifty.

Tetzel was a skillful peddler. He entered each town in a solemn procession and with great fanfare. He set up a cross in the market place and delivered a sermon in which he told the simple folk that their parents were suffering in eternal flames, begging for the release which their children could give. Then the preacher would say,

> As soon as the coin in the coffer rings,
> The soul from purgatory springs.

With such appeals the money would roll in.

When hardened sinners began returning to Wittenberg with Tetzel's indulgence letters and a smug feeling of spiritual security, Luther was deeply disturbed. The more Luther learned about Tetzel's methods, the greater became his alarm. On October 31st he spoke out.

19. Action and Reaction

This time Luther did not speak out with a sermon but a series of crisp bold statements which, he declared, he was ready to defend in a debate. These *Ninety-five Theses* were printed in Latin and posted on the door of the Castle Church in Wittenberg on the eve of the Elector's famous indulgence festival. Copies were also sent to key people elsewhere.

Luther's attack was religious. Though the money-grabbing features of the indulgence traffic did not escape his attention, he was concerned first of all with spiritual dangers. It is an error, he declared bluntly, to say "that by the pope's indulgences a man is freed from every penalty and saved." As a matter of fact, the pope does not have any power at all over purgatory. Even worse, indulgences give people a false sense of security, make them complacent and self-satisfied—an insult to both the holiness and love of God.

The Theses, though intended for scholars and officials, were soon known all over Germany and throughout much of Europe. The ordinary people who sensed its weight gladly received this protest. At first it was dismissed lightly by the pope and other high church officials. Soon, however, other theologians rushed into the fray with Luther and a lengthy struggle began. Pamphlets, sermons, and tracts began to pour from Luther's pen in a steady stream as he tried to explain his position.

The next summer Luther was ordered to appear before the papal representative, **Cardinal Cajetan,** at Augsburg. Luther went with many misgiving. He wondered whether his critics might be right when they taunted, "Are you alone wise and all the ages in error?" As debate made the issues clearer, he realized that he was being pushed more and more toward opposition to the church. What that meant all men knew too well. "I had the stake before my eyes constantly," he wrote later.

The interviews with Cajetan took place in October, 1518. The cardinal had been told to try to reconcile Luther to the church, not to argue or debate. Both proved impossible. Luther stubbornly asked to be shown where he was in error. Failing in this the cardinal thundered again and again, "Recant!" But the "shabby little monk" refused.

When Luther returned to Wittenberg, his position was both uncertain and dangerous. It was obvious that the church did not intend to hear him but to crush him. Measures to bring

this about had already been set in motion. Skillful theologians*
were working to undo him. There seemed to be only two alter-
natives—submission to authority or death. Only one man stood
between Luther and speedy judgment—Frederick, head of
Saxony. What was Frederick's attitude? Luther did not know

He expected the worst and was prepared to leave. "I am
expecting the curses of Rome any day. I have everything in
readiness. When they come, I am girded like Abraham to go
I know not where, but sure of this, that God is everywhere."
He thought of going to France. On the very day he had
planned to leave, word came that the Elector had written to
the pope on his behalf. The meaning was clear. Though no
disciple, the Elector was at least not going to be frightened by
papal power. Luther offered a grateful prayer and decided to
remain in Wittenberg and wait for the pope to act.

Then the pressure was relaxed unexpectedly for a time. Emperor Maximilian suddenly died in January, 1519. A new
emperor had to be elected. This was an important decision in
Europe's delicate political situation. The pope was eagerly bargaining for the choice of a favorable candidate. Frederick, as
one of the electors, had to be cultivated. There was even talk
of making his professor (Luther) a cardinal!

Meanwhile Luther was studying and writing. Books and
tracts came so rapidly that the printers could not keep ahead
of him. Five went to the printer in March and April (1519)
and two more in May. In all these works his development as
a reformer can be traced. His position was becoming more
and more radical. On the key question of the pope's authority
he was saying, "A command of the pope is binding only when
it is in accord with the glory of God."

20. Leipzig, 1519

Meanwhile a full-dress review of all the issues was brewing.
A learned scholar of Ingolstadt, **John Eck,** had been crossing
swords with Luther in print for a year. He had issued a challenge to public debate with **Carlstadt,** Luther's friend and disciple. Later on Luther himself was included. The place was
Leipzig; the time, 1519.

The Wittenbergers arrived in two open wagons late in June. There was considerable preliminary skirmishing about rules. After mass in St. Thomas Church and a long opening address by Duke George's secretary, the debate finally began. Carlstadt and Eck wrestled with each other for a week. Then Luther entered the lists. He was described by witnesses as of medium height and very thin from many cares and much study. Yet he was vigorous; his voice, clear and firm. His manner was friendly and sometimes even gay. He astounded men with his complete mastery of the Bible and his wide learning in theology. Eck was a heavy, square-set fellow with a loud, rather rough voice. He had a remarkable memory and a neat knack of talking himself out of difficult spots.

As Luther and Eck debated the authority of the pope, Eck suddenly pointed out that Luther's views were very close to those of the condemned John Huss. Luther denied the charge but during the lunch hour read again the acts of the Council of Constance. When he came back, he declared bluntly that the Council had condemned articles which were plainly Christian—for example, the statement that "there is only one universal church." Eck pounced on this and gradually pushed Luther to the damaging admission that councils as well as popes can and have erred. "Ach, the plague!" exclaimed Duke George.

To most persons the Leipzig debate was a victory for John Eck. There is no doubt that in branding Luther the "Saxon Huss" Eck had dramatized his heresy. Actually the debate was a turning point for Luther. Up to this point he had not been fully conscious of the gulf between himself and accepted Catholic teaching. Now he saw how far he had ventured on a new, lonely path in his search for biblical Christianity. He came face to face with Roman Catholic teaching on sin, grace, justification, the church, papal authority. He realized that he was drifting away. His conviction on the sole authority of the Bible, the church as the fellowship of Christian people, and the position of the papacy became much clearer. In the fierce struggle of debate the lines of conflict widened rapidly and were more sharply drawn.

V
Walking in a Lonely Way

21. Books and More Books

Luther returned from the Leipzig Debate and plunged at once into a period of amazing activity. There didn't seem to be much opposition but his enemies were busy in Germany and Rome plotting his downfall. They were sure that Luther had cooked his goose. On the other hand certain scholars and patriots in Germany came over to Luther's side and offered him support. Most people just waited to see what would happen.

Luther was hard at work. He had his regular duties of course, such as: his lectures at the university, his daily sermons for the monks, and his Sunday sermons for the town church. But most of all he was occupied with writing. Now that the battle was fairly joined, books, pamphlets, sermons, tracts, and letters poured from his pen in a torrent so that all the world could know what the quarrel was about. As no man ever before him, Luther took the public into his confidence. His basic religious ideas, as we have seen, had been worked out painfully, long before this. There were, however, a host of practical results. Now that the bars were down, Luther's mind and pen ranged over the whole field.

It is no exaggeration to say that Luther "made" the printing business in Germany. The art was less than a hundred years old, and books published in German up to 1517 had averaged about forty a year. But now Luther's own output was often much more than this. And of course many others began to write either for or against him. In 1520, 208 books were published in Germany, 133 of them by Luther himself. Luther did not write for money but to meet the needs in his great struggle. He seldom revised. He simply let the words and ideas tumble out. When a page was finished—especially if "a good strong anger stirred my blood"—he sent the sheets off to the neighboring printers. "I have a swift hand and a quick memory," Luther wrote. "When I write, it just flows out; I do not have to press and squeeze." The tremendous production from Luther's pen underlines the truth of this statement.

Books Published in Germany

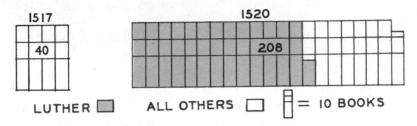

1517 40

1520 208

LUTHER ▢   ALL OTHERS ▢   ▯ = 10 BOOKS

In spite of the hurried preparation, the publications of 1520 were of the greatest significance. With almost furious intensity Luther was thinking out loud on some of the most vital issues of the Christian faith. Wherever he turned his attention, his new ideas revealed lost treasures or showed how far the Roman Church had strayed from the New Testament. It is not possible to review all of his writings, but here are a few with some snatches of his own striking words.

On Good Works: "If you don't have to be good and do good deeds in order to win God's favor and your salvation, what's the point of being good?" some people began to wonder. Luther's enemies said that his idea of salvation by faith cut away the main reason for living a good life. The church had suggested a whole series of "good works" which people were encouraged to undertake—"running to the convent, singing, reading, playing the organ, saying mass, praying matins, vespers, and other hours, founding and ornamenting churches, altars, convents, gathering chimes, jewels, vestments, gems and treasures, going to Rome, curtsying and bowing the knees, praying the rosary and the psalter." As you can see, Luther had little use for these things. People are trying, he said, "with their many good works, to make God favorable to themselves, and to buy God's grace from Him as if He were a huckster or a day-laborer, unwilling to give His grace and favor for nothing." This can't be done. "The first and highest, the most precious of all good works is faith in Christ." The person who has true faith will as a natural result do works of goodness, kindness, and love. In fact, Luther went so far as to say, any so-called good work which did not come from faith was really just hypocrsy.

53

On the Papacy at Rome: What is the church? According to Roman Catholic teaching the church was the great visible organization of Christians, led by their priests and bishops with the pope at the top. To be a Christian a person must belong to this organization. Luther disagreed completely. He quoted the Apostles' Creed where the church is described as "the communion (fellowship) of the saints." The church, he said, "consists of all those who live in true faith, hope, love." The church is not essentially an organization but "an assembly of hearts in one faith." The head of the true church, therefore, is not the pope or any man but Christ himself.

To the Christian Nobility: "The time to keep silence has passed and the time to speak has come." People everywhere hoped and prayed for a reformation that would sweep the corruption, greed, and worldliness out of the church. But the great church councils had accomplished nothing. Neither had the critics. In this stirring appeal Luther suggested that the princes of the various states, as Christian laymen, should do the job. This was a revolutionary idea. For hundreds of years people believed that a priest was superior to a layman. All earthly powers must yield to the authority of the church. But Luther's study of the New Testament led him to the belief that all true believers are equal before God. This distinctly Protestant idea is known as "the priesthood of believers." It means that a consecrated layman is as much a Christian as a priest and is in no way inferior.

"If a little group of pious Christian laymen were taken captive and set down in a wilderness, and had among them no priest consecrated by a bishop, and if there in the wilderness they were to agree in choosing one of themselves, married or unmarried, and were to charge him with the office of baptizing, saying mass, and preaching, such a man would be as truly a priest as though all bishops and popes had consecrated him." On this basis Luther argued that the lay princes should do for the church in Germany what the church seemed unable to do for itself. He wrote bluntly and sharply. He went right down the line discussing the abuses and suggesting remedies. It was an amazing attack. His deep indignation thrilled the souls of

Germans, both high and low. Here was the voice of a nation's anger crying out against insult, deception, and tyranny. Even his enemies admitted that there was much truth in his criticisms. Luther was not simply destructive. He did not just point out wrongs. He suggested steps that the princes should take to help their people.

Babylonian Captivity of the Church. To most people in Luther's day this seemed the most radical of all his books. The Roman Church had built its authority on its claim that the sacraments were the only channels of God's saving grace and that only priests could administer them. Luther examined the whole system and discounted it with one sweeping stroke. He argued that nothing could be a sacrament unless Christ established it. By this standard there are not seven Sacraments but two—baptism and the Lord's Supper. There is no such thing as a priesthood with special powers given by ordination. "We are all priests, as many of us as are Christians. The priests, as we call them, are ministers chosen from among us, who do all that they do in our name. . . . Ordination can be nothing else than a certain rite of choosing preachers in the church." Faith is the important thing. Therefore, "the works of monks and priests be they never so holy and arduous, differ no whit in the sight of God from the works of the rustic toiling in the field or the woman going about her household tasks. All works are measured before Him by faith alone." Luther even changed the meaning of the two sacraments he kept. He said they depended on the Word of God and not upon some special power of the priest.

On Christian Liberty. This little tract, which appeared in November of 1520, is much different from Luther's other writings of the same period. Most of them argued their points— sometimes in an angry time. This little gem is quiet, simple, deeply spiritual. Its main idea is this:

"A Christian man is a perfectly free lord of all, subject to none. A Christian man is a perfectly dutiful servant of all, subject to all." Since a Christian is saved by faith, he is free of all the usual fears and requirements. At the same time, the man who has found this liberty in Christ will want to show his gratitude in deeds of kindness and love. "Good works do not make a good man, but a good man does good works." Because God has given the riches of his love so freely, a Christian will try to "do all things which I know are pleasing and acceptable to such a Father, who has overwhelmed me with His inestimable riches."

22. Fire at the Elster Gate

While Luther was reading, thinking, and writing his books, the church authorities were not idle. In May the cardinals, lawyers, and theologians met at the pope's hunting lodge to decide on a course of action. A bull* was drawn up condemning forty-one of Luther's statements. "We can no longer suffer the serpent to creep through the field of the Lord. The books of Martin Luther which contain these errors are to be examined and burned." Luther himself was given sixty days to submit or be excommunicated.

Publication of the bull in Germany was placed in the hands of John Eck and another papal representative named Aleander. Almost everywhere they met with unexpected opposition and insults by the people. The bull finally reached Luther in October. Immediately he wrote a passionate reply, "I protest before God, our Lord Jesus, his sacred angels, and the whole world that with my whole heart I dissent from the damnation of this bull, that I curse . . . it as sacrilege . . . This be my recantation, O bull, thou daughter of bulls." Here and there Luther's books were burned publicly. But many people, including Elector Frederick himself, felt he had not been given a fair hearing or properly tried.

On December 10th the sixty days of grace allowed in the bull expired. About 10 o'clock that morning a group of professors and students from the university gathered outside Wittenberg's Elster Gate. A fire was started. Copies of the canon (church) law were thrown into it; also some theological* works and books by Luther's enemies. Then, praying and trembling, Luther stepped to the fire and threw in a little booklet. Only a few realized that it contained a copy of the papal bull. Afterward the students paraded around town in a wagon.

News of this dramatic little incident spread through Europe and made a tremendous impression. The whole medieval way of life had been built on canon law. In this simple act of burning a papal order, one man had defied the pope and made clear his break with the past. Luther himself spoke openly to his students of the possibility of his being martyred. Churchmen were horrified and denounced him furiously, but many others cheered. Christopher Scheurl wrote to friends in Wittenberg, "Everything is resounding with the deeds that have happened among you. Now either the Roman or the Saxon front must flinch." So it was.

23. The Diet at Worms

Of all the problems facing young **Emperor Charles V** as he came into Germany late in 1520, none was more vexing than the "Luther question." He himself knew what he would like to do. As ruler and a good Catholic he had no patience with those who defied authority, either civil or spiritual. Luther was under the ban of the church; the state's duty was clear. Luther should be punished.

But things were not quite that simple. Charles needed German support for his war with France, and many of the German princes (including some of the strongest) were sympathetic with Luther. Public opinion on all levels was divided. The pope's representative Aleander reported that nine-tenths of the Germans shouted, "Luther," and the other tenth, "Death to the pope." This was an exaggeration, of course, but many people were clearly for Luther, some strongly against him. Others, though not approving his heresies, agreed with a lot of his criticisms and did not wish to have him silenced. And then there was something else which complicated matters. At the coronation Charles had had to sign the German constitution which provided, among other things, that no German should be tried outside of Germany or outlawed without a hearing. How could Charles get his hands on Luther?

The great imperial Diet opened at Worms late in January 1521. All sorts of intrigue and maneuvering had been going on for months. All the pulling and hauling centered about one question: Should Luther appear before the council to be examined for his faith? Aleander, wily agent for the pope, did everything possible to prevent this. The Diet, he said, is a secular° tribunal and has no authority to judge a matter of faith. Luther has already been condemned by the church. That should end it.

Yet a determined minority in the Diet who wanted Luther to be heard could not be defeated. Finally it was agreed that he should be examined by learned men—to answer not to argue. If he refused to change, then the Diet agreed to act against him. On March 26th the imperial herald, Kaspar Sturm, arrived in Wittenberg to escort Luther to Worms.

On April 2nd, the Tuesday after Easter, Luther and a few friends climbed into the wagon which had been provided by the local goldsmith. The journey became something of a triumphal procession. People thronged "to see the wonder man who had been so daring as to set himself against the pope and the whole world." Some had little comfort to offer. "He will doubtless be burned to a powder in short order, as Huss was once burned at Constance."

As a matter of fact behind the scenes the emperor's party was making furious efforts to accomplish its purpose by frightening Luther away from Worms or persuading him not to come. Even the Elector Frederick was alarmed and advised Luther to stay away. But Luther wrote back to Frederick's adviser, Spalatin, "Christ is alive, and I shall enter Worms in spite of the gates of hell and the powers of darkness." Years later as an old man, Luther recalled, "I was not afraid. I suppose God can make a man that daring. I am not sure that I should now be so bold."

On the morning of April 16th trumpeters on the cathedral spire announced Luther's approach. About a hundred horseman, young Saxon noblemen, had ridden out to accompany the little procession into the town. The streets were so crowded that the party could hardly get to the house of the Knights of St. John where Luther was to stay.

The next day Luther was told that he was not to appear before a committee but before the Diet itself. About four o'clock he was led by the marshal through some back alleys (because the streets were so crowded) to the palace where the Diet was in session. Finally about six o'clock he was called. With four or five counselors he stepped into the presence of the assembled lords of the German states and the emperor.

There he stood a simple monk, son of a miner, with no resource but his own sturdy faith in the Word of God. Princes and representatives stared silently—some with hostility—at the determined figure. His large, dark eyes flashed and twinkled like stars, so that one could not look straight into them. Charles exclaimed, "That fellow will never make a heretic of me."

Finally the court official spoke out in a loud voice, "His Imperial Majesty has summoned you, Martin Luther, to find out two things: first, are you willing to confess that the books which have been circulated under your name are yours (he pointed to a pile of about twenty), and second, are you ready to renounce these books or part of them?" Luther's answer to the first question was "yes;" the second, he said, was more difficult since it "touches God and his Word." "I beg you," he concluded, "give me time to think it over." The request was granted, reluctantly.

24. "Here I Stand!"

The next day (April 18), Luther again appeared before the Diet. Gone now were the awe and timidity of the previous day. The question was asked again, and Luther replied with ringing voice in a speech that shook the world.

"Most serene emperor, most illustrious princes, most clement lords, if I have not given some of you your proper titles, I beg you to forgive me. I am not a courtier, but a monk. You asked me yesterday whether the books were mine and whether I would repudiate them. They are all mine, but as for the second question, they are not all of one sort." Some books, he pointed out, dealt simply with faith and life and were not condemned even by his enemies. These he could not retract. A second group dealt with evils in the church about which there was universal complaint. To recant them would open the door to worse tyranny.

A third group, Luther continued, contained attacks on individuals. He admitted that they were more bitter than proper but nevertheless were true. He went on, "If I am shown my error, I will be the first to throw my books into the fire. We should not begin, in our attempt to settle this controversy and

dissension, by condemning the Word of God. For that would bring down upon us a flood of unbearable evils, and it would be a very poor beginning for the reign of the young emperor. I commend myself to Your Majesty and to Your Highnesses with the humble plea that you will not permit my accusers to make me hateful in your eyes without cause."

After Luther repeated the address in Latin, the princes consulted. What had Luther said, "yes" or "no"? Both answers could be heard in his words. An official made an abusive address (apparently trying to break Luther's spirit). He reminded Luther of the authority of the church. He concluded, "Do you or do you not repudiate your books and the errors which they contain?"

The fateful parting of the ways had come at last. The religion of tradition and authority was set squarely against religion of personal conviction. Luther replied, "Since then Your Majesty and your lordships desire a simple reply, I will give you an answer without horns or teeth (that is, straight to the point). Unless I am convicted by Scripture and plain reason— I do not accept the authority of popes and councils, for they have contradicted each other—my conscience is captive to the Word of God. I cannot and I will not recant anything, for to go against conscience is neither right nor safe. God help me. Amen." (See picture on page 8.)

Tumult broke out. The Emperor arose and left in anger. Friends surrounded Luther and escorted him out with arms upraised in the sign of victory. "Al fuego, al fuego!" (Burn him!) hissed the Spaniards outside. Back at his room Luther stretched out his arms and exclaimed, "I am through! I am through!"

He would indeed have been "through" if Charles had had his way. The next day the Emperor called together the Electors and some of the princes to ask their advice. Before they could reply he told them his own viewpoint. "A single friar who goes counter to all Christianity for a thousand years must be wrong. Therefore, I am resolved to stake my lands, my friends, my body, my blood, my life, and my soul. . . . I will proceed against him as a notorious heretic, and ask you to declare yourselves as you promised me."

The edict* which the Diet now seemed ready to issue was delayed, however, by the threat of violence in Worms itself. Meanwhile Luther's "trial" continued, this time in a series of private conferences with church leaders. Hour after hour for almost a week, they talked with him in an effort, as Luther put it, to make him "unclench his fist and let go of the Bible." These friendly but almost frantic attempts to break down his will in the name of peace and church unity must have been extremely trying. Most of Luther's visitors were unable to appreciate the real difference in religious outlook between him and the old church. It apparently never entered the minds of any of them that he could be right. In the end they had to report failure.

Late in the morning of April 26th Luther quietly left Worms. About twenty horsemen accompanied him for a short distance from the town and sent him on his way home.

The Emperor and his advisers proceeded at once with the edict. The document was ready early in May. It reviewed Luther's case in a prejudiced way. It forbade everyone to have dealings with him of any kind, made it the duty of loyal subjects to seize the heretic and deliver him to the authorities, and made the buying, selling, printing, reading, or even possession of his books a crime punishable by death. Henceforth all books on religion were to be censored by the church, and publications of any kind had to receive the approval of the bishops.

Not till the end of May, when many of the members of the Diet had gone home, was the edict adopted. Could it be enforced?

VI
Chaos and Conflict

25. "In the Land of the Birds"

While princes and churchmen continued to argue at Worms, Luther and his companions jogged along quietly on the way home. At Eisenach the party divided; Luther and two others detoured by way of Mohra so that he could visit relatives. Not long after they had left their friends, a band of armed horsemen swept out of the forest and attacked the little party. Luther was dragged roughly from the wagon, pulled along by the riders until the rest were out of sight, and then put on a horse. They rode for hours constantly shifting direction to wipe out the trail. Finally about eleven o'clock at night the party crossed the clanking drawbridge into Wartburg Castle, high in the Thuringian mountains.

Luther's capture was so realistic that almost everyone thought it was the work of enemies. Albrecht Durer, the artist, wrote, "I know not whether he lives or is murdered, but in any case he has suffered for the Christian truth . . . O God, if Luther is dead, who will henceforth explain to us the gospel?"

Actually, when the Elector Frederick saw how things were going at Worms, he became afraid for Luther's life and had given secret orders to take him to a safe hiding place. Neither the Elector nor Luther himself knew the details which were arranged by a few trusted agents. Temporarily Luther was removed from the thick of battle.

The warden of the castle concealed Luther by "making him over" into a knight. For more than a week Luther was scarcely permitted to leave his rooms; meals were brought by two pages. He let the hair grow both on his tonsured (shaven) head and on his face. Soon he had a black, curly beard. He laid aside his monk's robes and dressed as a knight. After awhile he was able to roam through the woods and venture out into the neighborhood where he was known as Knight George. An attendant always went along, however, because the former monk and professor would sometimes forget himself, lay aside his sword. and pick up a book. In those days, of course, most knights did

not read books, and this would have been a dead giveaway.

From his window Luther could look out over the fair Thuringian hills. High up "in the land of the birds," to use his phrase, he found peace and quiet. Yet he was far from happy. "I wanted to be in the fray," he wrote. "I would rather burn in live coals than rot here alone." Part of his impatience was the result of illness. He was in pain and misery for weeks before his condition began to improve.

He was troubled also, however, by doubts. To Luther's lively, medieval imagination the Devil was always present. Night noises like the scurrying of rats, the fluttering of bats, the creak of limbs, and the sighing of wind through the recesses of the old castle were to him the work of demons. So he did daily battle with Satan. "Are you alone wise?" his conscience would ask. "Have so many centuries gone wrong? What if you are in error and are taking so many others with you to eternal damnation?" Again and again he felt like Elijah at Horeb. "Now, O Lord, take away my life!"

Equally disturbing were reports from the outside world.

The edict had been issued, and Luther was now an outlaw. New enemies rose up to attack the gospel. Albert of Mainz began to sell indulgences again. What steps would the church take now? What could be expected of the Elector Frederick? How were things going at Wittenberg?

From his spot "on the mountain" Luther tried to keep in touch with developments by correspondence. "Do not be downcast," he wrote to his young friend **Melanchthon.** "Sing the song which the Lord has commanded in the night; I will join in the song, and let us be anxious only for the Word."

Although Luther complained of being idle, this was hardly the case. In addition to his letters he was presently sending a variety of books and sermons to his friends for printing. One of these was a work *Concerning Confession* in which he came to the conclusion, from his study of the New Testament, that the Roman Church had no right to demand private confession of people. Repentance, he said, is not a routine but the free act of the believer who confesses his sins before his Lord.

Events at Wittenberg soon led Luther to write another book, *On Monastic Vows.* For a thousand years Christians had been going apart from the world into monasteries because this was thought to be a good way to win salvation. These differences, he now saw, have no basis in the gospel. The call of God can come to a man in any honorable occupation. Monkish vows are of no value because they are contrary to Christian freedom. Luther did not suggest closing the monasteries but would leave each person free to stay or to leave, marry, and take up a normal life. This book was a far-ranging attack on one of the most important parts of Roman Catholic life.

While all this was going on, Luther was working on translating the New Testament into German. This was the major product of his months of "imprisonment."

26. Riot at Wittenberg

Meanwhile the tempo of reform at Wittenberg began to increase sharply. In Luther's absence leadership fell upon Melanchthon, Carlstadt, and Zwilling. Except for indulgences the whole controversy up to this point had been largely a battle of theologians—so far as the man in the street was concerned. Suddenly in 1521 the principles became practical issues. Luther's colleagues at Wittenberg began to introduce a whole series of rapid changes. Priests, monks, nuns began to marry. Vestments° at services were changed or discarded. German was used in place of Latin. Meat was eaten on fast days. Many services were abolished altogether. The average German discovered that Luther's ideas made differences he could see.

What Luther learned about developments at Wittenberg at first pleased him. By the fall of 1521, however, disturbing reports began to reach his mountain hide-out. Carlstadt, though sincere, was given to extreme statements and drastic action. Zwilling was inclined to be even more fanatical. Conservative souls felt that changes should wait at least until there was some agreement about them. Others were impatient to be done with practices which they felt could no longer be justified by the New Testament. Frederick's adviser, Spalatin, commented, "What a mess we are in with everybody doing something else."

Early in December Luther made a secret visit to Wittenberg. He was alarmed. A harsh revolutionary spirit was abroad. He sensed that it would not stop at violence. His immediate response was a tract, *Against Riot and Rebellion*. "Preach, pray, but do not fight," he said. Force, he declared, must be exercised only by the proper authorities.

On Christmas Day Carlstadt conducted mass in a strange new way—partly in German, wearing just a black robe, the people receiving wine as well as bread. Some were clearly bewildered by these changes. Carlstadt and Zwilling had, on the basis of the Second Commandment, condemned images, pictures, statues, also music and organs in churches. Soon a series of riots broke out, led in part by the preachers. Mobs broke into churches, overturned altars, smashed pictures, disfigured gravestones. In the midst of all this turmoil some glib-talking laymen from nearby Zwickau suddenly appeared. They proclaimed themselves prophets of the Lord. Melanchthon was taken in and did not know what to do about their strange ideas. On top of everything else the town council passed an ordinance aimed at bringing about some of the social reforms Luther had advocated—for example, abolition of begging, public help for the poor, public education of the young.

Frederick was frightened. In February he issued instructions to the university calling a halt. "We have gone too fast," he said. A few weeks later he commented, "Everybody was at sea, and none knew who was the cook and who the ladle." Frederick was on the spot. He had to maintain order and at least make a show of keeping the laws of the empire. By those laws Luther was an outlaw. Catholic neighbors were threatening to intervene. Then suddenly amid all the confusion the town council sent for Luther to return.

It was perfectly clear to Luther that returning to Wittenberg was a dangerous step. The Elector might be unwilling or unable to protect him. Nevertheless he wrote, "I come to Wittenberg with a higher protection than that of Your Grace. I do not ask you to protect me. I will protect you more than you will protect me . . . This is not a case for the sword but for God . . . You are excused if I am captured or killed. As a prince you should obey the emperor and offer no resistance . . . If Your Grace had eyes, you would see the glory of God."

Luther reached Wittenberg on Friday, March 6, 1522. Beginning on Sunday he preached each day for a week on the problems which troubled the people. The whole life of a Christian man, he said, "is faith and love." Some things, like faith in Christ, are *musts* in the Christian life, "matters of necessity." But love "never uses force or undue constraint." "We must first win the hearts of people." His method, he declared, is to teach and preach the Word—and trust God to change men. Concerning all the non-essential things like burial forms, monastic vows, orders of worship, language, images, and the like people should have freedom of choice. It took him three years of constant study and reflection to reach his present position, he said. Ordinary men, unfamiliar with these matters, should not be expected to cover the same distance in three months.

Luther was listened to with tense excitement. His sermons were completely effective. A student who heard him commented about his cheerful face and rich voice and added,

"Everyone who hears him once, desires to hear him again and again, such tenacious hooks does he fix in the minds of his hearers." So, preaching patience and consideration, Luther restored order and moderation to Wittenberg.

27. Peasants on the March

But the reforming spirit and the violent temper were not confined to Wittenberg nor concerned only with religious matters. This was a revolutionary age, charged with explosive forces. Luther's mighty whacks at the follies and falsehoods of the traditional church had helped to stir up vast currents of unrest. Most notable was the **Peasants' War.**

Off and on for a century there had been serious uprisings among the peasants of Germany. Farmers in the Middle Ages had been held in serfdom°—practically as slaves. By Luther's day the farmers had a better position and more freedom. But there were many strains and much injustice resulting from new ways of doing business, new laws, and the new social order which was developing in Europe. For example, a sharp rise in prices (due to the introduction of gold and silver from America) and a series of famine years from 1490 to 1503 created a great deal of misery among the peasants.

Unrest often took the form of revolt. The symbol was the poor man's tied shoe (*Bundschuh*); the motto, "Only what is just before God." These peasant uprisings often had a religious quality. The demands today would seem just. They were, however, a dangerous disturbance of good order. Violence was met with violence as the authorities tried to deal with the rebellious mobs.

Forces from both sides brought Luther and the peasants together. Although he was concerned almost entirely with a religious reformation, his ideas of the priesthood of believers and Christian liberty could easily be interpreted in a political way. Besides in books like the *Appeal to the Christian Nobility* Luther had said some pretty revolutionary things himself. The peasant movements had combined a religious note with criticisms of the church which sounded a lot like Luther. Bundschuh rebels might hate the clergy, but Bundschuh banners usually bore Christian symbols.

The Peasants' War began in June 1524. Gradually through the fall and winter it spread over a large part of Germany. Two-thirds of the country was ablaze. At first the mobs of peasants seemed interested chiefly in raiding game and plundering monasteries and castles. There was comparatively little bloodshed. Then in March, 1525, a series of *Twelve Articles* appeared. These demands were rather moderate and at points sounded a lot like Luther. "The gospel is not a cause of rebellion and disturbance," said the introduction. In one petition request was made for ministers to "preach the Holy Gospel without human addition." Catholic princes said Luther was responsible for the whole trouble.

When Luther became aware of the violent temper of the peasants, he wrote a little tract in which he cautioned that under no circumstances should they resort to lawlessness and bloodshed. People have no right to use the sword against the established authorities. To the princes, on the other hand, he declared that the demands of the peasants were fair and just—were indeed God's judgment on their robbery, greed, and extravagance. For their troubles the princes had only themselves to blame. They had sown the seeds of their trouble.

The seething kettle boiled over when one of Luther's radical critics, a wildly imaginative preacher named Thomas Muntzer, managed to establish himself as leader of the peasants. He came to Muhlhausen and preached war. "Now is the time. If you be only three wholly committed unto God, you need not fear one hundred thousand. On! On! On! Spare not! Pity not the godless when they cry. Remember the command of God to Moses to destroy utterly and show no mercy. The whole countryside is in commotion. Strike! Clang! Clang! On! On!"

The peasants began a triumphant march late in April which reached a bloody climax in the battle of Frankenhausen on May 15th. The assembled princes and their troops took only 600 prisoners. Five thousand of the peasants were butchered. Elsewhere in pitched battles more than a hundred thousand were slain. The rebellion was broken, the peasants' bid for a better place in the new society crushed.

Meanwhile early in May Luther, greatly alarmed, wrote a wild tract *Against the Murdering Thieving Hordes of Peasants*. All the devils of hell, he said, had gotten into the peasants. They were in open rebellion, outside the law of God, laying waste the countryside. "Therefore," he said, "Let everyone who can, smite, slay, and stab. . . . remembering that nothing can be more devilish than a rebel."

Unfortunately the booklet did not appear at once when it might have seemed appropriate. It was delayed until late in June when the mobs had been pretty well hacked to pieces by the all-too-eager princes. The peasants felt with dismay that Luther had betrayed them. Many turned away from his leadership to seek some other religious home. Luther's furious words remain a mark on a Christian spirit which his friends cannot and his enemies will not forget. The whole experience gave Luther a deep distrust of the common man and an abiding fear of disorder.

VII

Building a New Church

28. Old and New

The middle twenties were years of decision and division in the reformation movement. Up to 1521 Luther had been the hope of the many groups in Germany who differed widely and were united by just one thing—the desire for change. But Luther was not prepared to be all things to all men. As the years passed and his broad principles were translated into practical policies, one group after another turned away from his leadership. Many, who applauded as long as he tore down the old, were not willing or able to follow when he turned to the task of building the new.

Many moderate Catholics, for example, who had clamored for a reform of the church, drew back when they saw that compromise was impossible and Luther would be forced out of the church altogether. They were not ready to go this far. There was an influential group of scholars throughout Europe who welcomed Luther's liberal views. But when they realized that he was still conservative about many things, they deserted him or were driven away. There were nationalists, patriots who saw in Luther the hope of a unified Germany. His *Appeal to the German Nobility* stirred their blood. But when it appeared that Luther was not a political but a religious leader, they lost interest and heart. The peasants who dreamed of a more just world and greater opportunity felt Luther had betrayed them when he denounced their rebellion. On the other side, there were religious radicals like Carlstadt who wanted to go the limit. When they realized that Luther was determined to follow a moderate, conservative course in reforming the church, they became dissatisfied and broke away.

In all of these cases the hostility was made worse by Luther's own temper. He found it difficult to use the soft answer which "turneth away wrath." Again and again his violent language and stubbornness repelled people who actually were for the most part in agreement with him.

Up to this point Luther had been first of all the critic and

MAP OF
GERMANY
in
LUTHER'S
day

reformer. The whole life and faith of the Roman Catholic Church had come under his review. Events had driven him to more and more radical positions. As the movement snowballed he had had to think through in the light of the New Testament such matters as indulgences, general councils of the church, salvation, good works, the nature of the church, sacraments, the mass, worship, social reform, monastic vows, and many others. His aim at first had been to purify and correct. The Diet at Worms had brought him to the parting of the ways. He was cast out of the church. Thousands believing as he did were ready to go with him. What then?

Tearing down is on thing; building is quite another. Luther stood, belabored and embattled, amid the dust and ruins of the corrupt old system, but what was to take its place? If the old church refused to change, what was to happen to the new life in Christ through faith? What was to become of the simple gospel of freedom and love and fellowship? Ordinary Christians were bewildered. If the old organization headed by the

73

bishops was to be discarded, who should take responsibility in the church? If the Roman mass was false, how should Christians worship and who was to decide? If monasticism was useless, what was to be done with the monks and nuns? Suddenly everybody seemed free to try out new ideas, to experiment— or to do nothing.

At first Luther had not been much inclined to do anything about these problems. Presently, however, he saw the need for action and threw himself with vast energy into the task of building. The foundations had already been laid in his earlier writings where he had developed a whole set of positive principles based on the New Testament. The task now was to apply these to the practical life of the church. He was assisted in this work by able men who had joined hands with him in the leadership of the Lutheran movement. Slowly but surely during the twenties a new church emerged. Let's see what it was like.

29. Authority and the Bible

Nothing marked this new church more than its different answer to the problem of authority. Who had the right to say that something was so or not—the Pope or some other human? In this argument the new church followed the lead of Luther. In his own experience Luther had come to realize the power of God speaking through his Word.

Arguments can sometimes be settled if both parties are willing to accept the judgment of an authority. Luther and his enemies never could get together because they disagreed on this basic point. He said the final authority in Christianity was the Bible, the Word of God. Catholics agreed but insisted that the Bible must be interpreted by the church. That meant "by the pope." To Luther this was simply putting the Bible under a human interpreter and could not be allowed. "The Word of God is above all the words of man," he said at Leipzig. "A simple layman armed with Scripture is to be believed above a pope or a council without it." "Do you think," he had said, "that your naked words can prevail against the armor of Scripture?" At Worms he demanded he be "convicted by Scripture."

The Roman Church needed an official interpreter because it had come to think of the Bible as a code of laws, a collection of religious truths which had to be understood properly and accepted if a man were to be saved. But long ago Luther had outgrown this idea. The Bible did not need an official interpreter to do its saving work because God was speaking directly to human hearts through its pages. Some parts might be more difficult than others, but it is possible for all men—whether highly educated or not—to hear the Father's voice and know the Redeemer's will.

Since this was the case, Luther soon saw that the Bible had to be gotten into the hands of ordinary Christian people. The church, he believed, is the result of the Word working in the lives of men. What better way to build the church of Christ could there be than to make the Bible available in a language men could understand? German translations had been printed as early as 1466 but they were clumsy, inaccurate, unfit to meet the needs of a fellowship where each believer was a priest, each man a reader of the Word. Luther decided that the only thing to do was to make a new translation of the Scriptures into the language of the common people.

Luther tackled first the job of translating the New Testament during his "exile" at the Wartburg. He must have worked with amazing ease and speed, for the whole task was done in about three months. Back in Wittenberg he began almost at once on the Old Testament. This was far more difficult. Because of many interruptions, the complete Bible did not appear until 1534. It was revised in later editions right up to the time of Luther's death in 1546.

Luther had done the New Testament single-handed. For the more complicated work on the Old Testament, he headed a committee of scholars. Few people can appreciate the difficulties in changing ideas over from one language to another clearly and accurately. "Good heavens," Luther wrote while working on the prophets, "how hard it is to make the Hebrew writers speak German!" Sometimes, he said, his "committee" searched for weeks to find the right word and could scarcely "finish three lines in four days." No one who glances over the smooth-flowing result can know the "humps and lumps" which had to be gotten out of the way with "sweat and toil."

Luther did not aim at word-for-word exactness but at a clear expression of ideas. For example, the meaningless but literal Hebrew phrase "the mouth of the sword" he translated "the edge of the sword." In the New Testament a strict translation of the angel's greeting to Mary (*Luke 1:28*) would be, "Hail, Mary, full of grace." But, says Luther, what does "full of grace" mean to a German? "He must think of a keg full of beer or a purse full of money. Therefore I have translated it 'Thou gracious one.'"

As a scholar Luther worked with his associates tirelessly to produce the most accurate translation possible. His Bible was superior in this respect to all that had preceded it.

His unmatched command of his native German was equally significant. He knew how people talked—the mother at home, the children in the streets, the common man in the market place. When he finished, Judea's hills, and people, and speech had come to Saxony and made themselves at home.

Luther's greatest asset for the work was his deep, spiritual sensitivity. He knew the Bible's religious atmosphere, for he himself had lived through it. He could draw on his own experience to find rich and reverent words through which the spell of the original laid hold upon his countrymen.

Critics then and since have found fault with one thing or another in Luther's Bible translation. ("Fine fellows!" he said. "They ought to try doing the job.") Yet the work was completely, brilliantly successful. By the time he died at least a million copies of the Bible had been sold though the price was about equal to twenty dollars.

30. Faith and Creeds

As we have seen, Luther's religious ideas had grown directly out of his own personal experience. His first protests had been made as an individual Christian. Even at Worms, though he had the sympathy of thousands, he spoke for himself. "A single monk, led astray by private judgment," Charles had said. In the course of ten years, however, thousands of people turned

their backs on the Roman Church and accepted the views which Luther had rediscovered in the New Testament. And so although he still had great influence, the Reformation was no longer Luther's private protest. The evangelical° faith was no longer his personal possession.

Luther's followers adopted in large measure the principles he had explained. They read the New Testament fervently, rejoiced in the love of God, and turned to Christ alone for salvation. But in the tense struggle for survival, there was need for clear-cut statements of faith. The people wanted some creed° to guide them.

The first of these guides came from Luther himself. They were the *Large* and *Small Catechisms* of 1529. Both were prepared to answer very practical needs. The previous year Luther had taken part in a visitation through the churches of Saxony. The Elector had approved this trip to find out what the conditions were in the church and to deal with problems. The visitors asked about congregational finances, forms of worship, the faith and behavior of pastors, the spiritual health of Christians. Luther was dismayed at what he found. Everywhere people were sunk in superstition and ignorance. They "seemed to have no knowledge whatever of Christian doctrine," he reported. They cannot recite the Lord's Prayer, the Creed, or the Ten Commandments. "Many pastors," he found, are "ignorant and incompetent teachers."

To meet this crying need Luther wrote his two catechisms. The larger appeared first and was intended for pastors and adults. Parts of it were read to congregations, and pastors used it to help them prepare sermons. More familiar and even more important was the *Small Catechism,* designed for children. Here the Christian faith was explained in clear, simple language. Luther followed the plan of earlier Roman catechisms in presenting the Ten Commandments, the Apostles' Creed, and the Lord's Prayer. But the richness of content and spirit were his own. To these three divisions he added sections on Baptism, the Lord's Supper, and some practical items.

Both catechisms became popular instantly, for they filled important needs. The *Small Catechism,* especially, was a superb

piece of work. Its glowing statement of a vital faith made it
widely useful and deeply loved. Young Christians in the Lutheran Church around the world down to the present have been
nourished by it. If you have not already started, you will
probably soon be studying it yourself. You will read that in the
introduction to the Lord's Prayer "God would . . . encourage
us to believe that he is truly our Father and that we are his
children." The First Commandment, you will learn, means
that "we should fear, love, and trust in God above all things."
And you may find, as millions of others, that few words that
can express more nobly than these what Jesus means to the
Christian:

    I believe that Jesus Christ, true God, begotten of the Father
       from eternity,
    And also true man, born of the Virgin Mary,
       Is my Lord;

Who has redeemed me, a lost and condemned creature,
Secured and delivered me from all sins, from death, and from
the power of the devil,
Not with silver and gold, but with his holy and precious
blood,
And with his innocent sufferings and death;
In order that I might be his, live under him in his kingdom,
And serve him in everlasting righteousness, innocence and
blessedness:
Even as he is risen from the dead, and lives and reigns to
all eternity.
This is most certainly true.

The catechisms were so widely accepted that after a while
they were regarded as basic Lutheran doctrine.

Of equal importance for the faith of the new church was
a statement known as the *Augsburg Confession*. It was given
this name because it was presented to the Emperor Charles by
the Protestants at Augsburg.

After the Diet at Worms in 1521, Charles had been so busy
with important troubles elsewhere in his huge empire that he
had had no chance to deal with the religious problem in Germany. Luther continued to work and preach. The Lutheran
movement grew in size and influence. At successive meetings
of the Diet no progress was made, but gradually two political
parties began to form. A meeting was held at Speyer in 1526,
but the religious question could not be settled. It was agreed,
however, that for the time being each prince was free to act
"as he would have to answer to God and the emperor." Then
for three years nothing further was done.

When the Diet assembled in 1529, again at Speyer, the Catholics, who were in a stronger position, moved to repeal the
decision of three years before. New regulations, most unfavor-
able to the "heretics," were passed. In this alarming situation
the evangelicals drew up a "protest" in which they declared
the new decrees were contrary to their consciences. For this
reason, they said they could not submit. "We fear God's wrath,"
they declared sturdily, "more than we fear the Emperor's ban."
It was this act which earned them the name of "Protestant."

At last in 1530 after ten years' absence, Charles was free to return to German soil. He presided personally at the Diet which was held in the city of Augsburg. The Emperor assumed an air of impartiality, hoping by patience and persuasion to bring the religious rebels back to the fold. But he was now at the height of his power and resolved to use the sword if mild measures failed.

Luther had hoped to go to the Diet. At the last minute, however, no promise of safe-conduct arrived for him so he was left in seclusion at Feste (Castle) Coburg in the Elector's territory. There amid the towers and rambling walls of this fortress high on a mountain he sat out—often with desperate impatience —the tedious negotiations at Augsburg.

His Imperial Majesty arrived early in May to the sound of booming cannon. When Charles dismounted, the papal representative, Campeggio, blessed the group. All of the princes instantly knelt, but the Elector John and Philip of Hesse refused to kneel and remained standing.

Then all went to the cathedral in a colorful procession. The two Protestants remained standing throughout the service. The next day the emperor summoned the Lutheran princes and demanded that they silence their preachers in Augsburg. They refused. Old Margrave George of Brandenburg looked the emperor in the eye and said, "Before I would deny my God and His Gospel, I would rather kneel down here and let you cut off my head." Charles was shocked and stammered in broken German, "Not cut off head! Not cut off head!"

Long negotiations followed in which every effort was made to outwit the Protestants. Warily they countered every move and steadfastly insisted on being heard. At last the Emperor agreed to let them present their case in public.

Hoping that this moment would come the theologians had been working on a document for months. The actual task of writing it was placed in the hands of Melanchthon. So great was the pressure that he was often discovered at his desk in tears. Numerous revisions were made as the winds of negotiation blew one way and another.

Melanchthon's purpose was to state what Lutherans believed

in as moderate a manner as possible. He still hoped for some kind of reconciliation with the Catholics. Stress was laid, therefore, on those points in which Lutheranism agreed with the old faith. Some very fundamental differences were altogether ignored—dishonestly, some felt.

Yet for all this it was a sturdy document. Luther, who at the Coburg saw an early draft, declared that "it pleases me right well." He admitted, however, "I cannot tread so gently and quietly." In the first part it presented Luther's characteristic teachings on faith, grace, justification, and so forth. The second part dealt with abuses in the church. Throughout the Confession Melanchthon stated strongly that the Reformation is a restoration of early Christianity.

The session of the Diet on June 25th opened at 3 P.M. The room and all the surrounding corridors and courtyards were crowded. The Protestant delegates rose to their feet as Chancellor Brueck of Saxony and Dr. Beyer stepped forward. For two hours they read this statement of their faith in German. At the end both a German and a Latin copy were given to the emperor. Five princes and two cities had signed. Five other

free cities signed at once. Others joined later. This was not
the act of churchmen but of laymen who boldly risked their
rule, their fortunes, and their lives for the sake of the gospel
they believed.

More negotiations and intrigue followed. Melanchthon, who
bore the brunt of these conferences, was not cut out for such
rough and tumble. By nature broadminded, peaceful, and
timid, he yielded so much at one time or another that he almost
gave away the whole Reformation cause. Luther, off at Coburg,
was almost frantic with concern. In the end the Emperor declared that the Lutheran articles had been shown to be false
and gave "to the Elector of Saxony, the five Princes, and the
six Cities" until the following April to reconsider, forsake their
heresies, and return to the true church. If they refused—the
sword!

That day in June, 1530 marked the end of an era. The
Augsburg Confession was the birth certificate of the Lutheran
Church. When those German princes, for themselves and on
behalf of their people, stood up and confessed their faith, the
ancient Holy Roman Empire came to an end. Now there were

two parties, one Protestant, the other Catholic. The document through which the princes spoke became, more than any other, the distinctive confession of all Lutheran churches in every part of the world.

31. Church Organization

Another problem Protestant leaders had to face was organization. In the Roman Church priests were under the authority of the bishop; administration was from the top down. In the new Lutheran Church you might say the responsibility was at the bottom in the self-governing, independent congregation—the fellowship of believers. In this democratic situation the pastor was not the representative of a great super-organization. He was simply a Christian like any other church member although set aside by choice of the congregation itself for the special duties of spiritual leadership.

Nevertheless an organization beyond the congregation was necessary. Who was to take the place of the bishop? What should be done with the income of monasteries which had closed? Luther had been against uniformity in nonessential things, such as forms of worship, but to simple people this variety often seemed like confusion. Who should decide what was to be done? Above all who was to see to it that ministers lived uprightly and preached the pure gospel?

Luther's answer was to call upon the princes, as leading Christian laymen, to take the lead in guiding the church. This was nothing new. For hundreds of years the rulers of the lands had exercised great authority in the Roman Church. Luther looked to them not as princes but simply as influential members of the church. Unfortunately in time the arrangement put the various Lutheran churches almost completely under the control of the rulers.

In Saxony the Elector appointed a commission to investigate conditions, handle practical problems, and make recommendations. The visitors, Luther among them, went through the land inquiring into finances, forms of worship, the faith and behavior of pastors. What they discovered was depressingly bad. Many of the ministers were former priests who had become "Lutheran" with little or no change in beliefs or way of living. Some did not know the Ten Commandments or the Lord's Prayer. One congregation complained that its minister preached on the art of making beer. In one area only ten out of two hundred clergy were found to be living moral lives. One minister served a Lutheran parish and a near-by Catholic church at the same time!

Since most of Saxony had gone over to the evangelical° way, many felt it was proper to use severe measures, even death, to suppress opposition. Luther, however, still objected to the use of force in matters of faith. Priests who could not make the change to the new church, therefore, were pensioned (if they were old) or dismissed (if they were young). Only the worst ministers could be removed since there were none to take their places. To meet the needs until young men could be trained, laymen were appointed as emergency teachers. For a while merchants, stonemasons, teachers, printers, even sextons filled in. It was to help leaders like these that Luther wrote his catechisms and many volumes of sermons. He wanted ministers to preach not about "blue ducks," as he said ignorant ones sometimes did, but about the gospel. It was a generation before the new church got the kind of ministry it needed—educated, spiritually alert, morally upright.

32. New Ways of Worship

Worship is much closer to ordinary Christians than either doctrine or organization. For many this *is* religion. Here is something they can see and grasp. So the Reformation became more than an argument about words when it began to alter the familiar ways of worship.

To appreciate the change it is necessary to know what had been going on in the Roman Church. The chief service was called the "Mass." Through the centuries it had become a dramatic and impressive form. Every device was used to add beauty and dignity to the worship—elaborate vestments,° lights, music, incense, chanting, symbolic action. The complicated ritual° was always said in Latin. When the priest elevated the communion elements at the altar, it was thought he was repeating Christ's sacrifice on Calvary. Going to Mass was a good work which would help in saving of a man's soul. Because the bread and wine were now the precious body and blood of our Lord, it was thought dangerous to risk spilling the wine (blood). For this reason it had become the Catholic practice for lay people to receive only the bread in communion. The wine was drunk only by the priest. This was called "communion in one kind." The average worshiper attended a service which he could not understand and in whch he seldom took part. He was a spectator. Yet he went in awe and reverence to witness a mystery and to see God in a brilliant ceremony.

Luther had made an attack upon the Roman Mass in his *Babylonian Captivity* (1520). As people began to accept his ideas, more and more demanded the reform of the service. In all these matters Luther felt men should be free to follow their own taste or conscience.

Soon pastors here and there were making changes as they saw fit in the ancient order of the Mass. Some were radicals who had little taste or judgment. They seemed to want to get rid of everything Catholic just because it was Catholic. Vestments were discarded, beautiful church windows smashed, images overturned, organs demolished. One former priest jauntily conducted service with three feathers in his beret. And if few went to this extreme, there certainly was a lot of fumbling and groping in the new church.

For some time Luther seemed reluctant to take a hand in this matter. Eventually, however, the confusion led him to prepare several booklets about worship. His own position—and it became that of his followers—was conservative. He had grown up in the Roman church and loved the meaning and beauty of the Mass even though he realized much of it needed changing. First he simply purified the old service but kept it in Latin. Then he realized ordinary worshipers did not notice such changes. So in 1526 he came out with a service in German (his "German Mass").

As the result of Luther's suggestions and the work of leaders elsewhere, the Lutheran Church began to develop its own forms of worship different from those of the Roman Church.

One of the most obvious changes was the practice of communion "in both kinds." In other words, laymen began to receive the wine as well as the bread. At first this was looked upon as a sensational departure. For a while people were free to commune either in the old way or the new.

A second striking change was the use of German, the language of the people. For the first time uneducated Christians were able to understand clearly all that went on in the service. As the people listened, they discovered that the Mass was no longer a sacrifice. Instead it was a service of thanksgiving and of fellowship both with God and with other believers. They went to church not because it was a duty or a good work but because they sought the privilege of God's presence. Christ and his saving work were the central themes.

The use of the common language made possible still another important feature of Lutheran worship, participation by the congregation. In the Roman Church most of the Mass had been monopolized by the priests and the choir. The people were spectators. Now they became active participants through responses, hymns, and prayers.

On such matters as vestments, candles, altars, altar cloths, crosses, incense, vessels, pictures, organs, stained glass windows, and so forth Luther and his followers were conservative but free. They felt that such things are "not important to faith and conscience." A Christian should be at liberty to use or not use them so long as he does not go against Scripture. On the other hand, they told radicals who wanted to pitch all these "popish inventions" out the window, that the Christians had the right to use art and music in worship. In general, however, Luther's followers did simplify the glittering service of the Roman Church. Lutheran preachers, for example, often replaced the elaborate vestments of the priest with a simple black robe.

There are two other features of Lutheran worship that really ought to be mentioned. One is the striking new emphasis upon

The Reformation Emphasized

preaching. In the medieval church the ceremony of the Mass had become more important than the sermon. There was preaching, but much of it was terribly poor. Ignorant priests translated the official Latin sermons in a dull way into the language of the people. More scholarly preachers simply showed off their knowledge. Popular preachers entertained the people with silly stories. Luther told how one of them was not above crowing like a cock in his sermon. One time the sexton, who had fallen asleep, woke up with a start and, thinking the preacher had shouted "The Lord be with you," gave the response, "And with Thy spirit." "Preachers waste their time," Luther said, "in serving up ridiculous rubbish . . . silly twaddle." As a result "the Bible was covered up, unknown, and buried."

Luther made the preaching of the Word central in worship. "The chief and greatest aim of any service is to preach and teach God's Word," he said. Each man must know and study the Bible, but how is he to understand it if it is not explained day in and day out! The reformers at Wittenberg used the pulpit as a major way of teaching religion. There were three or more services on Sundays and at least one each week-day. Where people had been used to watching a ritual they could not understand, they now participated in a service planned not only for praise but also for spiritual enrichment.

Luther himself was one of the great preachers of the Christian church. Twenty-three hundred of his sermons are known today; many others have disappeared. Like all preachers, Luther was ineffective at times. But at his best—which was often —he was dynamic, earnest, persuasive. "God, the creator of heaven and earth, speaks with thee through His preachers," he said. He approached the task in this spirit. Yet his sermons were down-to-earth, simple, sparkling with humor, illustrations, the language of common life.

The most important thing about preaching in the new church was what it emphasized. *"Praedicamus Christum—we preach Christ,"* is the way Luther put it. In the old church angels, saints, popes, and the Virgin Mary had seemed more important than Christ. Now he stood out clearly and alone—the Savior and Lord. This was a vital change.

A second important feature of Lutheran worship was the use of music by the congregation. Chanting° had been standard practice in the Roman Mass. The Lutheran Church also used this method of leading the service mainly because the church buildings did not lend themselves to reading aloud. But Luther insisted upon simplifying the music so that people could understand. When the service was put in German, he adapted the old music to the new language.

Luther was not a professionally trained musician, but he could sing and play the lute. More than that he had appreciation and a deep enthusiasm for music. It is, he said, "a fair and lovely gift of God which has often wakened and moved me to the joy of preaching." He praised it "as second only to the Word of God." Since he had, as he put it, "no use for cranks who despise music," he accepted it freely as an aid to worship. His attitude was much different from other reformers, such as Zwingli and Calvin, who limited music in the service or abolished it altogther. Luther helped prepare the way for the marvelous development of choral music which later reached a high point in the work of J. S. Bach.

The most important musical reform of all came in congregational singing. In the Roman Church most of the singing had been done by the priest and choir. In the Lutheran Church each believer was a priest and worship called for active participation. For this reason Luther converted whole portions of the service into hymns for the congregation. In addition, as early as 1524, he brought out a collection of hymns, some of which he had composed himself. Most of his compositions were based on Psalms or earlier Latin hymns, but he treated all of this material with a free hand so that it breathed the fresh spirit of the new faith. The most familiar of his hymns is the great song of the Reformation "A Mighty Fortress is Our God." It is a rugged, defiant hymn of faith. Others also are still in use —"Out of the Depths I Cry to Thee," "Lord, Keep Us Steadfast in Thy Word," for example.

Lutheran people not only learned to sing at church but also at home and in times of trouble. A Roman Catholic enemy declared that "the hymns of Luther killed more souls than his sermons." The Reformation swept across Germany on a wave of congregational song. This was, in any case, a wonderful new development in worship.

33. New Ways of Christian Living

The Bible and evangelical faith together were soon responsible for the appearance in the new church of a different idea about Christian living. For a thousand years the church had taught that the ideal Christian life was that of the monk. The home and daily occupations were good and necessary but definitely not as holy as a life of unmarried poverty, meditation, and prayer apart from the world. Such a life was the surest way to salvation. There were, therefore, two standards of life and conduct. Those who were not cut out for the heroic life of the monk or nun themselves paid tribute to the ideal by making pilgrimages to saintly shrines, by giving gifts to monasteries, and by devoting their own children to the system.

Daily life for the pious Catholic was likely to involve a rather elaborate round of masses, confessions, prayers (rosary, etc.). Fasts on the one hand, saints' days and festivals on the other were scattered through the calendar to remind the Christian of his heritage and religious duties. Piety centered in the priest and the church. All of these activities were believed to be good works which contributed to a person's merit before God.

The new Protestant view of the Christian life grew out of its basic principle. "How can a man get right with God?" Not by anything he does, Luther had discovered. You cannot win God's favor; he gives it freely. You have to trust God, commit yourself to him, humbly accept his love. Good works, therefore, are not to help us earn forgiveness but come as the result of it. A Christian does not live a good life in order to win God's favor but in gratitude for God's love. Just to say this may make

Images   *Rosary*   *Relics*   *Indulgences*

the difference seem slight, but actually it is an enormous one.

The system of merit of the Roman Church had been used as a way of developing character. A man tried to be good because he was afraid of what would happen if he were evil. But, said Luther, no man, even the best of us, can be so good before God as to merit any reward. We are all sinners. Well, said Luther's enemies and even some of his friends, why, then, be good? Why not just give way to temptations and let God forgive?

This, said Luther and the new church, is a complete misunderstanding. Christians are called to the highest type of moral living. The motive, however, is not the fear of punishment but gratitude for God's kindness. Christians must always be good. But they must always remember not to trust in their virtue or boast proudly about it before God. Instead they should respond humbly and gratefully to the love he has shown in Jesus Christ our Lord. "Good works do not make a man good, but a good man does good works," said Luther. "When God in his sheer mercy and without any merit of mine has given me such unspeakable riches, shall I not then freely, joyously, whole-heartedly, unprompted do everything that I know will please him?"

Because of this position the new church got rid of a lot of old practices: masses, prayers, pilgrimages, indulgences, fastings, contributions, confessions were no longer looked upon as ways of salvation. When any of them was retained, it was simply as an aid to devotion.

Instead of a lot of things designed to save one's own soul. the new church laid stress on constructive, helpful service to others. "I will give myself as a sort of Christ to my neighbor as Christ gave himself for me," Luther said. In sharing the common life and serving those in need, the Christian demonstrates

hallenged

Votive candles   *Fast Days*   *Pilgrimages*   *Incense*

that Christ has taken possession of his heart. "The good things we have from God should flow" on through us "to those who have need of them." This is "what Christ did for us. This is true love and the genuine rule of a Christian life."

One thing the new Protestant attitude did was to wipe out completely the distinction between sacred and secular,* especially in the matter of a person's work. All honest vocations are sacred. Schoolteachers and cooks, shoemakers and housemaids going faithfully about their duties do a work more pleasing to God than monks singing psalms. Our Lord worked as a carpenter. The Virgin Mary cleaned house and washed kettles. Peter was a fisherman. Even the shepherds at Bethlehem went back to their sheep. So Christians must labor. God works thus through human hands, lowly tasks are sacred, and all our life is blest.

At the same time the reverse of this is also true; all believers are priests. The work of praying before God and ministering to others is not limited to the specially ordained few. It belongs to all Christians without distinction. The minister is not set apart from other believers by an indelible quality; he is selected by the congregation for his special ministry of the Word. At the Lord's Supper "we all kneel beside him and around him, men and women, young and old, master and servant, mistress and maid, all holy priests together, sanctified by the blood of Christ."

This was a revolutionary doctrine. With one bold stroke it swept away the sense of inferiority, spiritual or otherwise, which had afflicted all who were engaged in the so-called secular occupations. It gave an honest dignity to all toil and enabled the humblest laborer to do his daily task to the glory of God and with a high sense of calling. So the Protestant looked at daily life with new eyes—not as something to be escaped but as a normal experience where God reveals himself in love and grace and where one may serve him quietly and with honesty.

Nowhere did these ideas bear more important fruit than in the Protestant idea of the home and family life. For hundreds of years in the old church men and women had given up marriage, entered monasteries or the priesthood, and thought they were better for doing so. Now Luther and his followers declared bluntly and simply that "the true service of God does not consist in the unmarried life," that on the contrary the normal joys and responsibilties of a home are well-pleasing in God's sight.

In fact in the new church the home replaced the monastery as the training ground for character and the school of Christian living. Whereas the highest ideals of the Christian life had been exemplified in the monastery with its detachment from the world, its ascetic° ideals, its quiet routine of work and prayer and worship, and its yearning for saintliness, now in the Protestant church the ideal was shifted to the home. Here amid the daily necessities of work, cooking meals, washing clothes, digging the garden, meeting the neighbors, disciplining and educating children, sharing love and sorrow, joy and anxiety the Christian is called to follow Christ in trust and love. The monastic brotherhood became the family circle; cloistered worship, family devotions; and monastery schools, catechetical instruction by the head of the household. Catholicism had made the church itself an almost exclusive center of worship and devotion. Protestantism added to this the home as an equally important center of Bible reading, worship, prayer, and Christian instruction.

VIII

Luther the Man

34. Martin and Katie

No one set the example for a Protestant home more fully than Luther himself. Early in the Reformation movement he had attacked the notion that being unmarried was especially holy. As his teachings and this idea in particular spread through Germany, monks and nuns began to leave the monasteries and convents in droves. It was a crime punishable by death to help monks or nuns escape. But one day in 1523 a respected merchant of Torgau concealed a dozen nuns in some empty fish barrels and drove them out of a near-by cloister in his wagon. Two years later Luther had managed to arrange the marriage of most of these nuns. There was one, however, a plain, proud, sensible girl for whom he had not found a husband. And at twenty-six she was rapidly slipping beyond the age of marriage. Her name was Catharine von Bora.

Suddenly in June 1525 Luther married Katie von Bora. He had repeatedly declared that, while he thoroughly approved the marriage of ministers, he did not himself intend to take the step "because I daily expect the death decreed to the heretic." He married, he said, "to spite the devil" (in other words, to defy what he felt was a false teaching of the church) and to please his father.

The wedding was a private affair with just a few witnesses. Two weeks later a public celebration was held with a service at the church, a big dinner, a wedding folk dance at the town hall, and then another banquet.

If there was little romance in the courtship, a deep affection and sincere appreciation soon developed in the marriage. "Katie, you have a husband that loves you. Let someone else be empress," he wrote once. And when she became ill, he exclaimed, "Oh, Katie, do not die and leave me."

Luther had to make a lot of changes. He admitted that before marriage he had not made his bed or changed it for a whole year. "I worked so hard and was so weary I tumbled in without noticing it." Katie took over, cleaned house, and presently with great skill assumed the management of things. This was no easy task, for Luther's income was small, his responsibilities large, and his generosity unlimited. Katie was just the kind of wife a man like Luther needed.

The Luthers had six children, one of whom died as a baby. In addition they raised a handful of children of relatives and regularly entertained a series of student boarders and visitors. Sometimes there were as many as twenty-five in the home—and almost no privacy.

Over this noisy, busy, restless household Katie was boss ("My Lord Katie," he would call her), and Luther was master. Sometimes he was stern in discipline or sharp in speech. Once when Luther had been talking at length (he was always talking—sometimes profoundly, sometimes hilariously, always interestingly) Katie interrupted. "Doctor, why don't you stop talking and eat?" "I wish," he snapped, "that women would repeat the Lord's Prayer before opening their mouths."

On the whole, however, it was a lively, happy home. Luther, though busy, enjoyed his family. "Hans is cutting teeth," he wrote, "and beginning to make a joyous nuisance of himself." A few years later he observed, "God must be kinder to us and speak more gently to us than Katie does to her baby. Katie or I would not gouge an eye out or knock the head off our own child—and neither will God with his children. He gave his only Son to make us trust him."

As might be expected, there was a deep religious note in the family's life. Even visitors—and there were many—were expected to conform to custom. Study of the Catechism, prayer, and family devotions were regular features. Hymn singing was common.

When Luther's daughter Magdalene was fourteen, she became seriously ill. Luther was utterly shaken by the possibility of her death. "O God," he exclaimed, "I love her very much but if it be thy will to take her, I submit to thee."

Then he asked, "Magdalene, my dear little daughter, would you like to stay here with your father, or would you willingly go to your Father in heaven?" She answered, "Dear father, as

God wills." Luther struggled to accept God's will thankfully and at last prayed that God would take her. She died in her father's arms. When they buried her, Luther said,

"You will rise and shine like a star, yes, like the sun. . . . I am happy in spirit, but the flesh is sorrowful and will not be content, the parting grieves me beyond measure. . . . I have sent a saint to heaven."

35. The Mark of Genius

The Reformation story from 1530 on is complicated and confusing. For Luther himself, however, these years were fairly quiet. The movement was no longer his personal possession. His was always an influential voice but no longer the only one. At Wittenberg, amid family and friends, he continued to teach, preach, and write. These were in many ways the happiest years of his stormy life. What kind of man was he?

Luther possessed a brilliant and independent mind. The stamp of genius was upon it. His memory was astonishing; his powers of concentration, unequalled. Many of his most important writings were the product of but a few days' intense labor. His energy was enormous. Even in these later years when age and illness took a heavy toll, he continued to work at a furious pace. His writings fill more than a hundred large volumes.

Little of this material was carefully revised, and he himself confessed that he was often wordy and repeated himself. Yet he was wonderfully effective as a writer because the man himself was on every page. He was at once human, colorful, homely; now humorous and playful, now furious in anger; passionate in debate, rugged and serene in meditation. One moment he could speak in tender tones little short of poetry and the next moment give way to furious denunciation.

When the plague appeared in Wittenberg in 1535 there was thought of closing school. Luther wrote to the Elector: "I observe that the said youths rather like the outcry about the plague; some of them get ulcers from their school bags, others colic from the books, others scurvy from the pens, and others gout from the paper. The ink of the rest has dried up, or else

they have devoured long letters from their mothers and so got
homesickness and nostalgia; indeed there are more ailments of
this kind than I can well recount."

On those who tried to unite Protestants and Catholics by
glossing over important differences: "I see they think this is a
comedy of men instead of a tragedy of God and Satan, as it
is. . . . I write with rage and indignation against those who
trifle in such matters."

While the Diet met at Augsburg in 1530 he described a "diet"
of the crows meeting beneath his window at Feste Coburg.
"They fly to and fro at such a rate and make such a racket day
and night that they all seem drunk, souses, and silly, I wonder
how their breath holds out to bicker so . . . Their hall is roofed
with the vault of the sky, its floor is a carpet of green grass, and
its walls are as far as the ends of the world." They plan, he
suspects, "a vigorous campaign against wheat, barley, oats,
and all kinds of corn and grain, a war in which many a knight
will do great deeds."

Luther's faults, like his virtues, are clearly revealed. As he
became older he grew disturbingly intolerant. He dismissed

those who disagreed with him in the most violent language. Ill health, disappointment that more did not accept his reforms, and disgust with moral laxity made him increasingly bitter. Even friends and colleagues did not always escape his short temper and abuse.

He was a man of extremes and contradictions. He was often melancholy and depressed, yet a wholesome lively humor and a steady cheerfulness abound. He could flail his enemies with furious anger and yet be as gentle and tender with children as a woman. His faith was simple but his arguments sometimes dull and obscure. Although radical in his age, he was essentially a conservative.

Perhaps all this is simply saying that he was refreshingly human. His personality was warm, engaging, attractive. He might bully and domineer his associates, but they could not escape his magnetic influence and they loved him. Wherever he went people of all position flocked about him. His lively manner, hearty laugh, ready sympathy, and complete lack of pretense were instantly appealing. Melanchthon said once, "I would rather die than separate myself from this man."

His honesty was unquestioned. Luther did not possess the slightest streak of sham. "Reckless of consequences, of danger, of his popularity, and of his life, he blurted out the whole truth, as he saw it, 'despite all cardinals, popes, kings, and emperors, together with all devils and hell.'" Luther had nothing to hide. His private life was public knowledge. When he spoke it was from the heart, without restraint or calculation.

Luther was brave. In 1527 when the plague sent most of the Wittenberg faculty fleeing, Luther stayed like a good pastor to minister to his people. At Worms he had stood unbroken and without fear before the mightiest leaders of the church and empire. On a half-dozen occasions he expected death, but would not tremble. He was ready to obey God. He had perfect confidence in God's power to save him or to claim him.

Luther's courage, like almost every important trait of his personality, grew out of his rocklike trust in God. In his lifetime he covered a vast range of problems and spoke out on many practical matters. Yet he was actually concerned with just one thing—a man's relation with God. He was, above all, religious. So for all his vast learning, he came to God like a child to his heavenly Father. He called himself "a child and pupil" of the essentials of the gospel as stated in the Catechism. "I have not yet passed the primary class," he said once. "It irks me not a little that I, a doctor, with all my learning should willy nilly stay in the class with my little Hans and Magdalene and go to school with them." So through the years he battled with his doubts and detractors, with the devil and despair, and learned to walk with God by faith. As he himself wrote,

> A mighty fortress is our God,
> A bulwark never failing;
> Our helper he amid the flood
> Of mortal ills prevailing.

36. End of an Era

From 1540 on Luther was increasingly a sick man. Neglect in the monastery and his punishing labors had taken their toll. Among his illnesses were indigestion, kidney stones, rheumatism, ulcers, abscesses in the ears, and heart disease. Yet he never relaxed in his work. In the last year of his life he lectured at the university, preached and published eleven books or pamphlets.

In the winter of 1545-6 he was asked to help settle a bitter quarrel which had broken out between the counts of Mansfeld. In the middle of the winter he made the journey to Eisleben in slow, open carriages. His letters home to Katie were cheerful and, as always, lively. By February (1546) such progress had been made that Luther was writing about returning home. On February 17th an agreement was finaly signed settling the difficulties. That night, however, Luther complained of faintness and pressure around the heart. About two o'clock in the morning his friends were aroused in alarm. Luther had taken a turn for the worse. Luther knew what was happening. "Reverend father," said one of his friends, "will you stand steadfast by Christ and the doctrine you have preached?"

"Yes," whispered the dying man.

Four days later Martin Luther was buried in the Castle

Church at Wittenberg where in 1517 he had posted some theses that shook the world.

*   *   *   *

Although less than three decades had elapsed between the posting of Luther's Ninety-five Theses and his death, tremendous changes had been wrought by the Reformation throughout all of Europe. Luther's most permanent influence outside of Germany was in Scandinavia where the new faith received a ready welcome.

Ruler of Denmark at the beginning of the Reformation was Christian II. He was a man of much learning who seemed to have a genuine interest in the welfare of the people. However, in his effort to increase both his own and the people's power at the expense of the nobles, he clashed with the church (Roman) and in 1523 was forced into exile.

Under his successor, Frederick I, Protestant ideas swept through Denmark. Among the leaders was the vigorous young Lutheran preacher, Hans Tausen, who presently became the king's chaplain. Civil war followed Frederick's death in 1533 and the religious issue hung in the balance.

When Christian III became king in 1536 it was clearly as a Lutheran (by conviction) and in response to the desires of the people. In July 1537 Luther's able friend and associate John Bugenhagen arrived in Copenhagen. His first duty was at the coronation. Everyone caught the meaning when in a splendid ceremony the new king and queen were crowned not by the Catholic Archbishop of Lund but by Lutheran Pastor Bugenhagen. Quite as important was the service a few weeks later when he presided at the ordination of seven new "superintendents" or "bishops" for the Danish Lutheran Church.

There is no question that personal and political factors played a large part in the Danish Reformation. The Catholic bishops had had as much political as spiritual authority. Many were unworthy, greedy, and secular. Unrest and dissatisfaction with the church provided an opportunity for the Reformation. In a single generation and with little opposition Lutheranism was adopted by the people as a whole.

Since Norway and Iceland were at this time under the Danish

king, the Reformation came to them as changes were made in the home country.

Sweden also had been part of Denmark but when Christian II came to the throne, Sweden was in revolt. The king finally subdued the rebels but lost the war by his own treachery. Stockholm had surrendered after siege on promise of mercy. At the urging of the Archbishop of Upsala, however, the king seized ninety of the leading nobles of the realm and had them led into the market place where one by one their heads were chopped off before the horrified people. This "blood bath" united all Sweden against Denmark and even against the Roman Church.

Revolt broke out under Gustaf Vasa who presently was elected King of Sweden. He was a popular choice but faced an almost impossible task. The expenses of government were more than twice the royal income. Two-thirds of Sweden was owned by the church and most of the rest by the nobles—and all claimed tax-exemption. A solution to the king's public problem seemed at hand in the new Protestant faith with which he had some private sympathy.

Olaf and Lars Petersson, the sons of a blacksmith, had been sent to study in Germany and had come under Luther's influence. When they returned to Sweden, they found an ally in an influential theologian and churchman Lars Andersson. The king now made Andersson his private secretary. Olaf Petersson became a great popular preacher and writer (probably translated the New Testament) who used his influence to spread Lutheranism in Sweden.

Matters came to a head in 1527 when Gustaf, desperate for funds, proposed to take over all church properties not actually needed by the church. After three days of argument the Diet at Vasteras yielded to the king; there was no other way. The Swedish church lost much of its property and became subject to the king. Steps were taken to improve the parish ministry and eliminate financial abuses. Otherwise there was little change. Forms of worship, old ceremonies, vestments, and customs remained as they were. Even the organization of the church under bishops was not altered. Lutheran ideas were everywhere abroad in the land, however, and gradually through the years the Church of Sweden became clearly and unmistakably Lutheran. In this most peaceable of reformations not one person lost his life for his religious convictions.

Finland, at this time part of Sweden, became Lutheran by the same process.

✿ ✿ ✿ ✿

Meanwhile the forces Luther had unleashed had shaken the whole structure of the Holy Roman Empire. In 1530 the Emperor had threatened Lutherans with the sword. Yet for years he could do nothing about it. Conference after conference was held; complicated and prolonged negotiations were carried on. Whereas Luther had once stood alone, now there were many spokesmen for the Protestants. Nothing could be accomplished; between Lutheran and Catholic the gulf had become too wide to be bridged or overlooked.

Meanwhile princes on both sides formed military alliances. Fortunes ebbed and flowed with the changing pattern of European politics. Open warfare did not break out until 1547, a year after Luther's death. The first victories went to the Emperor. Suddenly a few years later the Protestant princes were able to reorganize themselves and almost succeeded in capturing Charles.

At the Diet at Augsburg in 1555 the religious question was finally settled. Lutheranism was given official recognition as a legal religion in the Holy Roman Empire. Charles, broken and defeated, surrendered his crown and retired to a monastery. The Religious Peace of Augsburg was almost the same agreement which had been reached at Speyer in 1526. Peace might have come a generation sooner if Charles had not insisted fanatically on trying to maintain the unity of a Catholic German empire.

37. Zwingli

Luther's trumpet blasts were heard not only in Germany but throughout Europe. Once the dike was broken, criticism and reform swept over the old Roman Church in a flood that could not be stayed. In almost every country Protestants of one kind or another appeared.

The first were at Zurich, Switzerland where the leader was a brilliant and eloquent preacher named **Ulrich Zwingli** (1484-1531). Although Zwingli was Protestant in general outlook, he differed from Luther at one important point. He went much farther in making the Bible a rule and guide in the church. Luther had said that Christians were free to do what the Bible did not forbid. He had retained, therefore, many familiar practices. Zwingli, however, said Christians could do only what the Bible commanded. Since the Bible said nothing about crosses, beautiful windows, organs, and liturgy, the Zwinglians got rid of them all.

We have already seen how the princes in Germany took a hand in helping Luther. In Switzerland where there was considerably more independence, the matter was soon brought before the Town Councils. In these Public Disputations° both sides would be argued and a decision given. Invariably the outcome favored the Protestants. At the disputation in Zurich in 1523 the mayor announced that they were there so that anyone could refute the so-called errors of Master Zwingli "by Holy Scripture freely, boldly, and without fear of punishment." On that basis there was little contest. Zwingli carried the day. As the meeting broke up one Protestant commented, "Where were those who wanted to burn us and had the wood piled at the stake?"

All Switzerland was astir with religious excitement. Wherever Protestants were strong enough to bring matters to public debate, they were victorious. Some cantons,° however, remained stoutly Catholic. The upshot was war. Protestant

advance was halted by defeat at the bloody battle of Kappel
in 1531. Zwingli himself, who had gone along as chaplain, was
wounded, captured, and burned as a heretic.

38. Geneva and John Calvin

After the disaster at Kappel, the chief center of Protestant
activity passed from Zurich in German Switzerland to Geneva
in the French section of the country. The leader was a French-
man, **John Calvin**, who had come to the city in 1536 and set
about at once re-organizing its life.

His ideal for Geneva was a *theocracy*, that is, a community
ruled by God. He set out to create a city where people believed and lived as Christians. The ministers formed the *Venerable Company*. Every week they met to study the Bible,
discuss their faith, and review conduct. Upon each one of the
Venerable Company was laid the duty of criticizing and in-
structing the others.

Even more important was the *Consistory*, in which both ministers and laymen were represented. Its duty was "to keep
watch on the life of everyone." The task was taken literally,
for Calvin aimed to create a community of saints. The consistory was to see to it that every citizen met the highest standards of Christian faith and conduct. It sat as a regular court to
hear complaints and impose punishments. Many a sinner was
required to kneel and cry out to God for mercy. Most citizens,
who were used to rough justice, expected to spend some time
in prison. But they found the tyranny of the consistory hard
to accept.

Cases which called for something further in the line of discipline were passed on to the *Town Council*. All medieval communities had a lot of petty laws regulating personal conduct, but they were seldom enforced. Under Calvin, however, these rules were extended and applied with astonishing thoroughness. Dancing, playing cards, cursing, and swearing were, of course, forbidden. Claude de la Ravoire, who swore while out hunting, was given three days in prison on bread and water and forbidden to hunt again. Three young workmen received similar treatment for over-indulging in pie. Etienne Buffet, who said that neither God, the devil, the magistrates, nor ministers would keep him from beating his wife, was sent to prison. The color and quality of clothing were regulated by law as was the way women could fix their hair. Parents were forbidden to use certain names in baptizing their children. Innkeepers were to see to it that no guests stayed up after nine o'clock.

In Calvin's Geneva not only right living but also right believing was insisted upon. Any differences of opinion about religious matters were punished severely. There were many cases through these years, but the most famous was that of **Servetus,** a doctor-turned-theologian. Servetus admitted the divinity of Christ but denied the doctrine of the Trinity. In 1553 he was condemned to be burned by the Catholic Inquisition at Vienne but managed to escape. Foolishly he went to Geneva where he was recognized, tried all over again, and again sentenced to burning. As Servetus faced death, his last words were, "Jesus, Thou Son of the eternal God, have mercy on me!" He might have been allowed to live if he had been willing to say, "Jesus, Thou eternal Son of God."

Such stern measures were typical of sixteenth century Europe. But it was the relentless efficiency with which they were enforced in Geneva that aroused the anger of many persons. In one five-year period in this little city of sixteen thousand people, there were at least fifty-eight executions and seventy-six banishments. Calvin was cordially hated by many. By 1555, however, those who opposed him were completely broken and cowed into submission. From then until his death in 1565 he was undisputed master of the city.

39. Calvinism

This dark side of the Reformation in Geneva should not, however, obscure other achievements. Under Calvin—and chiefly because of him—the city became a refuge for Europe's oppressed Protestants and a great center of influence and leadership. At one time or another almost every important Protestant leader of Europe outside the Lutheran fold spent some time under Calvin. To train a new leadership he established an "Academy" which trained skilled, dedicated leaders to go back to their own lands to preach and teach and, if need be, to suffer and die for the gospel.

To Calvin the Bible was always the supreme authority. Like Zwingli, he thought of the Bible as a law book to be followed in detail. It lead him to transfer to the Christian Sunday all the Old Testament regulations for the Jewish Sabbath. Worship was held in plain meeting houses without vestments, organs, bells, candles, colored windows, or ritual. Since these things were not commanded in the Bible, they were forbidden. The chief hymns were Psalms from the Bible. The service consisted of Bible-reading, prayers, hymns, and above all the sermon. The Lord's Supper was celebrated regularly in a simple fashion.

Calvin's most important book was a systematic statement of the Christian faith called the *Institutes of the Christian Religion*. It was first published in 1536 when Calvin was just twenty-six. Luther's ideas always grew out of the experience of salvation through Jesus Christ. Calvin, however, started with the fact of God whose power and will he regarded as fundamental in the universe. This sense of being chosen by the Lord to accomplish his will, gave Calvin and his followers a dignity which refused to quail even before the mighty of the earth. They were the church, the elect of God, his chosen ones.

So Calvin's followers were the makers (as we shall see) of a new age. Work was to be done with high seriousness and to the glory of God. And as for governments, Calvin said that when princes or magistrates go against God's law, Christians not only may but also must rebel. So men of his spirit battled the forces of darkness and in a later age put down tyrants and fashioned democratic governments.

Calvin was a giant in an age of great men. Though frail of body and often weakened by disease, he drove himself relentlessly to perform his duty under God. He had "a cold heart and hot temper, a clear brain, an iron will." To his associates he was a warm and friendly leader, steadfast and invincible. His intellect won their admiration but his character claimed their affection. His work was to give to Protestantism a courage to endure, a zeal to conquer, a clarity of thought, and an integrity of character.

40. Huguenots under the Cross

Nowhere was Calvin's influence felt more strongly than in France. He spoke as a native, of course. Through personal contacts at Geneva and through hundreds of letters all the austere power and charm of this amazing man were felt by hundreds who became his disciples. His courage and his passion alike became theirs. By the middle of the century much of the best leadership of France had become Protestant. The first synod or meeting of churches was held in Paris in 1559.

What happened in the next forty years is one of the dreadful chapters of modern history. The Protestants, or **Huguenots** as they were now called, gradually became objectors not only to the king's Catholic faith but also to the king's authority. Religion and politics were mixed together in a gigantic, bloody struggle between the freedom-loving Huguenots and the royal power. War after war swept across France. Huguenots smashed images but were in turn slaughtered by the hundreds. At Vassy, for example, in 1562 a congregation at worship was attacked by soldiers of the powerful Catholic Duke of Guise. Hundreds were massacred. On St. Bartholomew's Day in August 1572 a general order was issued by the court to slay the heretics. In the wild manhaunt which swept France, twenty thousand Protestants were slaughtered. These were but incidents in the struggle which brought the whole country to the brink of ruin. Neither Protestant Huguenot nor Catholic League was able to win sufficiently to break the dead-lock.

In 1589 King Henry III of France was assassinated. Next in line to the throne was Henry of Navarre, who for years had been the leader of the Huguenots. Could Henry make good his claim and break the civil war? By sheer personal courage, wearing "a terrible white plume," he led his men to victory in battle. But he could not take Paris, make peace, or win the throne in a France which refused to have a "heretic" for a king. At last in 1593, sacrificing convictions for country, he became a Catholic. "Paris was worth a mass," he said. In 1598 he published the Edict of Nantes giving full liberty and legal rights to Protestants and leaving in Huguenot hands more than two hundred towns.

41. Reformation in the Low Countries

When Philip II, the brooding and fanatical king of Spain, inherited the Low Countries, he resolved to bring the people back to the Catholic fold or "so to waste their land that neither the natives could live there nor should any thereafter desire the place for habitation." He almost succeeded in this awful threat. Among the Dutch resistance became both a patriotic and a religious necessity. They wanted liberty and their Calvinist faith armed them with a heroic will not only to suffer but even more to fight tyranny.

The struggle was long and savage. The patriots, whom the king's regent called "beggars," wore the title proudly. In 1567 Spanish troops were ordered into the country to deal with rebellion and heresy. Hour after hour, day after day the courts ground out executions. More than ten thousand were killed in six years. To add to the misery the Duke of Alva who was governor imposed taxes that were ruinous to a commercial people like the Dutch. Panic swept the country. In this period of thirty or forty years some four hundred thousand Netherlanders left the country.

The hopeless cause was rescued by the organization of the "Sea Beggars." The Dutch discovered they could seize the coastal towns and occasionally carry the war to the Spanish garrisons. Alva reacted with "Spanish fury." In storming Zutphen he ordered his troops "not to leave one man alive or one building unburnt." The Spanish could win on land; the Dutch, on the sea.

Gradually Spanish control was thrust off though the fighting continued for years. In 1581 the northern provinces separated from the southern (Belgium) and established the independent Dutch Republic. A vigorous form of Calvinism was established. The people, however, who had suffered so much for so long, had acquired a hatred of oppression, a tolerance for differences, and a love of freedom which soon made their country a haven for the persecuted from all of Europe.

42. Knox and the Scotch Reformation

At the time of the Reformation Scotland was a rough, barbaric country, one of Europe's distant frontiers. Its people would almost rather steal and fight than eat. "So long as I may . . . steal, I will never work," says a Scotsman in a current poem. The Reformation changed that. It made them a sober people under the discipline of John Calvin.

The revolution was almost bloodless. Evangelical preaching, together with political and social discontent, won the people to the Calvinist faith. In 1560 the Parliament adopted a Confession and abolished the pope's authority.

The man who shaped this revolution more than anyone else was John Knox, "a good fighter and a good hater." For the most part he had guided the Reformation from a distance. In 1547 he had been captured by the French and made to serve time as a galley slave (rower) in the fleet. Upon his release he had lived as a religious refugee in England and Geneva. Knox had seen the fury of Catholic persecution and had been hardened by his own sufferings. With unswerving passion he desired to rid his country of "the poisoned and pestilent papists." His ideal for Scotland was the same as Calvin's at Geneva —a theocracy.* The church was organized under elders or

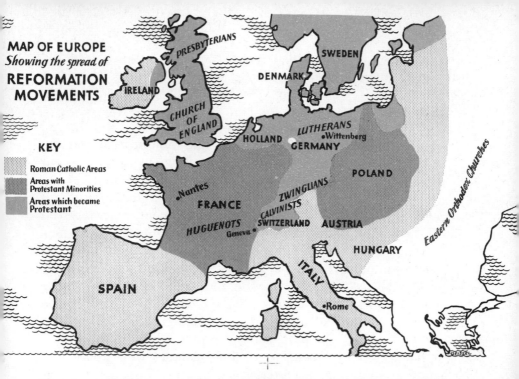

MAP OF EUROPE
Showing the spread of
REFORMATION
MOVEMENTS

KEY

Roman Catholic Areas

Areas with
Protestant Minorities

Areas which became
Protestant

PRESBYTERIANS

IRELAND

CHURCH
OF
ENGLAND

HOLLAND

SWEDEN

DENMARK

LUTHERANS
•Wittenberg
GERMANY

POLAND

•Nantes

FRANCE

ZWINGLIANS
CALVINISTS

HUGUENOTS   SWITZERLAND   AUSTRIA
Geneva•

HUNGARY

SPAIN

ITALY

•Rome

Eastern Orthodox Churches

"presbyters" who were elected by the people. This Presbyterian church in Scotland became the best expression of Calvin's ideas outside of Geneva.

The new Catholic queen, Mary Stuart, was feminine, French, and foolish. She was irritated by the authority of the ministers. "I see that my subjects must obey you and not me," she complained to Knox. "God forbid," he replied. "My concern is that both princes and subjects obey God."

Mary had high hopes of some day becoming the Catholic Queen of England as well. Repeatedly she clashed with the fiery Knox, who told her bluntly that "if princes exceed their bounds, madam, they may be resisted and even deposed."

"What are you within this commonwealth?" she cried once in a rage. To which the preacher replied, "A subject born within the same, and though neither earl, lord, nor baron, yet has God made me a profitable member of the same."

Mary, betrayed by her weakness of character, was deposed by Parliament in 1566. Scotland became independent, Protestant, and Presbyterian.

X

Changes in England

43. Reform Begins in England

In the stormy sixteenth century the Reformation was the result of many forces, not all of them religious. Nowhere was its beginning more political and personal than in England.

This does not mean there was no religious agitation. Luther's ideas and **Tyndale's** English New Testament were received eagerly, but most people showed little desire to adopt the new "heresies." What started the English Reformation, however, was nothing more than the personal desires of the king, **Henry VIII.** This strong, intemperate monarch could not get the pope's consent to his divorce. So he decided to "take over" the church. Parliament obediently passed a series of bills which made the king "sole protector and supreme head of the church and clergy of England," cut off all contact with Rome, and appropriated some monasteries.

All this was not done, of course, without protest. But Henry simply chopped off heads. He had no intention of changing the faith of the English Church. He simply wanted to be free of Roman authority so that he himself could manage at least the church's outward affairs. The service was put into English and some priests married, but old forms were maintained and bishops continued to run the church.

Protestantism took root during the reign of Edward VI (1547-1553), Henry's son. The leading reformer, Thomas Cranmer, prepared the *English Book of Common Prayer*. A broad but clearly Protestant confession of faith was adopted. Edward died suddenly and was succeeded by Henry's daughter, Mary, a Catholic. She married Philip II of Spain and determined to bring England back to the Roman Church. The combination of Spain and Catholicism was thoroughly unpopular. Mary tried persecution. Many Protestant leaders were imprisoned or killed. Said Bishop Latimer to a friend when they were led to the stake for burning, "Be of good cheer, Master Ridley and play the man. This day we shall light such a candle, by God's grace, in England, as I trust, shall never be put out." He was right. Englishmen never forgot "Bloody" Mary and their country's bitterest reign of terror.

During her sister **Elizabeth's** long reign (1558-1603) the English (or Anglican) Church took shape. It was a conservative body much after the Lutheran pattern. Many familiar elements that the people loved were retained—like the old liturgy, richer for being in English. Native English patriotism and the Queen's firm but moderate policy drew people to the national church.

44. Puritans and Kings

By the time "good queen Bess" died in 1603 the Reformation was firmly established in England, but not all the religious problems had been solved. Elizabeth's policy had been to move slowly and make as many people as possible happy with the established church. To keep things under control, laws were passed about details like vestments (the special robes of ministers), kneeling to receive the Lord's Supper, the use of rings at weddings, placing organs in churches. It was felt that

it was very important to have uniformity in these outward details.

Actually opinion was far from uniform. Many Protestants who were more radical wanted to go much farther in "purifying" the church of its "popish" practices. Most of these **Puritans** were spiritual children of John Calvin. Sober, honest, and self-reliant, they opposed not only Catholicism but also despotism.

The big struggle of the century was to see whether king or parliament should rule England. Religion got mixed up with this political struggle, however, because in the minds of many people bishops and kings were necessary for each other. The king, they said, ruled by "divine right." King James' favorite saying was, "No bishop, no king." This was the position of the Anglican Church.

The Puritan party, which was more democratic, was against the divine right idea. Bishops, they said, were both unscriptural and Roman Catholic. When they discovered that their bishops played along hand-in-glove with the monarchs, the Puritans rebelled.

The first king after Elizabeth was **James I,** who came down from Scotland. He is remembered chiefly because the **Authorized** or **King James' Version** of the Bible was published during his reign. His high-handed ways with Parliament and his tactless irritation of the Puritans (he issued a *Book of Sports* to be played on Sundays!) aroused deep resentment. His son, **Charles I,** went even farther in trying to rule the church and do away with Parliament. Some Puritans, feeling their cause was hopeless, sailed across the ocean to New England by the thousands. Most of them stayed in England, of course, to fight out their battle with the king.

Soon there was civil war. When the folly of the king made them strong enough, the Puritans prepared the Westminster Confession and tried to make the church Presbyterian. Charles lost his head (literally) in 1649 and a Puritan government under "Lord Protector" **Oliver Cromwell** took over. When Cromwell died, however, the people were ready to try a king again. **Charles II** (1660-1685) was determined to rule and to

114

get rid of all who opposed him. The jails overflowed with Puritans. Tens of thousands suffered. The next king, James II, was an out-and-out Catholic who aimed to make Catholicism the national church again. Englishmen might not agree on their Protestantism, but they were united in objecting to "popery." So in 1688 **William of Orange** of the Netherlands and his English wife, Mary, were invited to become the new sovereigns. James fled. Three months later the Toleration Act was passed. It gave basic, personal religious freedom to all Protestants in England. Different kinds of worship could now exist side by side.

So religious peace came at last to England. There were, of course, later developments, but never again was religion so clearly a central issue in English public life. The wildly changing fortunes of this bitter contest had caused tens of thousands of hardy, conscientious refugees to seek their freedom in the colonies across the Atlantic. There they made mighty contributions to a new society. The struggle for religious liberty was a critical chapter of the English people's fight for freedom.

45. Separatists

Not all of the Puritans who joined in this struggle stayed within the official church. Gradually they got out or were driven out and organized congregations of their own. Together they formed the Dissenting or Independent or Separatist or Non-Conforming wing of English Protestantism. Although they gradually formed into separate church groups, they had many things in common.

For one thing they did not like the formal worship of the Anglican Church. Their own services were plain, free, and informal. They were all influenced strongly by Calvin's views although some made more room for what they felt was the direct influence of the Holy Spirit. Services were held in plain meeting houses without such "popish" inventions as altars, crosses, candles, vestments, pictures, or even organs. The services consisted of prayer, Scripture reading, psalm-singing, and preaching. Services lasted as long as three or four hours, and there were often two of them on Sundays.

The Puritan preachers were well-educated but usually more vigorous in manner than was customary in the Anglican churches. "How often," said a critic poking fun at them, "have you seen a preacher heat himself, beyond the need of any vestments? Throwing off his cloak, nay and his gloves too, as great impediments to the holy performance, squeaking and roaring beyond the example of any lunatic . . . while the people with great amazement have gaped upon him?" But the people liked the sincerity and enthusiasm of their ministers more than the stuffy formality of the Anglican priests.

The Puritan groups also believed that the Christian life was a sober thing without much room for self-indulgence or silly pleasures. They objected to the low morality of the nobility and insisted upon the highest standards of personal purity. Drunkenness, immodesty, stealing, gambling, laziness, card playing, dancing, fancy dress were all condemned.

The dissenting groups all shared the heavy hand of persecution. The law required that all Englishmen belong to the official Church of England and conform to its faith and practices. The Puritans refused and, of course, got into lots of trouble. They were forbidden to meet for worship but met anyhow as a

matter of conscience—and posted guards to warn when the authorities approached. Some meeting places were equipped with extra doors so the pastors could escape if the services were suddenly raided. Those who were caught were sometimes given brutal treatment.

Persecution was at its worst during the reign of Charles II. After awhile, however, most people became sick and tired of oppression and the spying and suffering that went with it. Many public officials simply gave up trying to enforce the law. It was obvious that police methods could not make everybody conform to the official church.

46. Congregationalists

In 1582 a Dissenter named **Robert Browne** wrote a booklet entitled *A Treatise on Reformation without Tarrying for Any.* So "without tarrying for any" he and his followers separated from the official church and got rid of bells, fancy vestments, pictures in windows, organs, and everything else which seemed to them to be Catholic.

The most important thing about these Independents, however, was their idea of church government. The Established Church had claimed that the traditional organization under bishops was the only system approved by the Bible. After awhile the Presbyterians began to make the same claims for their system. Now the Independents argued that both were wrong—that the church should be governed only by the congregations themselves. They said that groups of Christians who meet together for worship and communion with God, either with or without ordained ministers and liturgies, are truly the church. For this reason they were called **Congregationalists.** Their system had a decidedly democratic slant. The New England Pilgrims were of this group.

47. Anabaptists and Baptists

Not all the dissenters were Congregationalists. Some were Presbyterians. At the close of the reign of Charles I they had almost succeeded in making their system the official government of the English Church just as it was in Scotland. But they failed in this and eventually became another non-conforming group outside the English Church.

To understand the origin of the Baptists it is necessary to go back to the beginnings of the Reformation on the continent. The appeal of the Reformers like Luther and Zwingli to the Bible started many people thinking about religious matters on their own. In Zurich in 1522 two men named Grebel and Manz felt that Zwingli had not gone nearly far enough in applying the Bible. This new group differed in several ways from the type of Protestantism being developed by Luther and Zwingli.

For one thing they began to question the value of baptizing babies. The sacrament, they believed, should be given only to those who had made up their own minds to join the church. So they refused to baptize their own children and baptized themselves over again. Their enemies called them **Anabaptists** (which means re-baptizers).

The really important thing about the Anabaptists was their idea that church and state should be entirely separate. Catholics and the other Protestants all thought of the state as Christian since most of its citizens were members of the church. The church was to them a great institution including all the citizens of the state.

But this is wrong, said the Anabaptists. The church is really made up only of the true followers of Jesus Christ. All others— the lukewarm and skeptical—may be citizens of the state, but they have no place in the church. Moreover the state itself is not Christian. It goes to war although Jesus taught men to love their enemies and it makes citizens take oaths. The only proper arrangement is for the church to be separated entirely from the state so that Christians can live according to the Sermon on the Mount.

Needless to say these ideas seemed dangerous. Occasionally the Anabaptists resorted to force, but in the main they were quiet, peaceable folk drawn chiefly from the lower levels of society. Everywhere they were hounded by the most horrible persecution. Heresy and treason were the usual charges, and they suffered from Catholic and Protestant alike. They were hunted down like wild beasts. They were buried alive, drowned, mutilated, burned, or killed with the sword. Theirs is one of the saddest chapters in the whole story of the Reformation.

Under the strain of constant suffering it is not surprising that wild ideas appeared among the Anabaptists. Their best-educated leaders were constantly being killed off. In the main, however, the Anabaptists were workmen with little formal education but a thorough knowledge of the Bible which they studied earnestly. Because they had no use for learning, government, or industry, they seldom became anything but farmers. They were content with a quiet, God-fearing, upright life according to the Scriptures.

Following the first wave of persecution the Anabaptists, especially of the Low Countries and Germany, were organized somewhat by a former priest, **Menno Simons.** He gave his name to an important group of Anabaptists in both Europe and America, the **Mennonites.**

About 1607 a group of English dissenters, fleeing persecution, came in contact with the Mennonites at Amsterdam. They studied their teachings and became convinced the Mennonites were right in refusing to baptize babies. Eventually this group came back to London and in 1611 established the first **Baptist** church in England. Baptist congregations soon spread all over England and grew rapidly in numbers. They share most of the major viewpoints of Protestantism while insisting upon adult baptism. They are like the Congregationalists in organization, placing authority in the local group. Above all they have stood staunchly for religious liberty and complete separation of church and state.

The most famous Baptist of the century was probably **John Bunyan.** He had to spend more than twelve years in prison because of his dissenting views. While there he wrote *Pilgrim's Progress,* one of the world's great religious books. When the officer asked why he didn't agree to stop preaching and be obedient to the authorities as Paul was, he replied, "But Paul was put in prison. There is more than one way to obey. We can obey by doing everything we are told, and we can obey by refusing and suffering what is done to us."

48. John Wesley

It often happens in a nation or an organization or even in a family that when the pressure of some great crisis is past everyone lets down. Wartime patriots sometimes make poor peacetime citizens. Convictions held fervently in time of struggle sometimes slip quietly away in days of peace. So it happened in the English churches following the settlement of 1689. Christians let down. The industrial revolution was changing the face of England. People were being gathered together in vast grimy communities around the mines and factories. But the church, indifferent and at ease with its privileges, did not follow these lost sheep. Life was brutal and coarse on all levels of society. The church had neither the courage to rebuke the sins of the mighty nor the conviction to preach the gospel to the lowly.

All this was changed by a hardy, little preacher named **John Wesley.** While at Oxford University he was the leader of a small group which tried methodically to study the Bible, serve the lowly, and live the Christian life. They were dubbed **Methodists.** In 1738, after a period of spiritual struggle, John was "converted." But what then? His urgent, warm-hearted appeals to the spiritual life seemed so terribly enthusiastic to most self-satisfied English ministers that they would not have him in their churches. He and his friends were called "fanatics."

John Wesley's mission to England began one Sunday in April, 1739, when he listened to his eloquent friend **George Whitefield** preach in the fields to the people of Bristol. What Wesley saw convinced him. The next afternoon he stood up on a rise of ground and preached to about three thousand men. This was an enormous break with his own orderly and educated past. So strong was tradition, he confesses, that "I should have thought the saving of souls almost a sin if it had not been done in a church." But the ice was broken. And so day after day for more than fifty years Wesley preached indoors and out wherever he could find an audience.

What John Wesley preached was not especially new, but it seemed new in his day because so many people had forgotten what Christianity was really about. They had forgotten

120

that getting right with God involves changing one's life so that it conforms to God's will. They had settled for a faith that was just so many words. Wesley thought that becoming a Christian means being "born again" and entering a new life with God. It means being spiritually alive, sensitive to the love and goodness of God, aware of his gracious presence. Moreover it means growing in holiness of life.

As Wesley freely admitted, he and his Methodists shared "the common, fundamental principles of Christianity." Two things marked them as different from other church members in their day: first, the enthusiastic feelings of joy and gratitude with which they accepted their personal salvation; and, second, their conviction that if Christ is in a man's heart, he simply has to make a difference in his life.

49. Mission on Horseback

Wesley soon realized that his mission was to the rough, uneducated, and often abused working people of England. By the tens of thousands they had drifted beyond the reach of any church. These miners and factory hands, these gambling,

ENGLISH PROTESTANT STREAMS

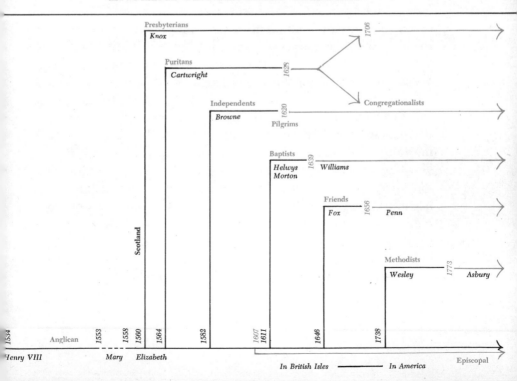

brawling, drunken dwellers in the slums, were 'the poor and forgotten of the earth. But to Wesley they were children of God with souls to save. Here is one of the amazing things—that this refined Oxford scholar should become the evangelist to "the other half" almost over night. Up and down England, Ireland, Scotland, and Wales he traveled 225,000 miles by foot, carriage, and horse on roads far worse than we can imagine. Most of his reading was done on horseback. In snow and sleet and rain he went about meeting people, talking, persuading, praying, converting, and preaching. Always preaching. In his lifetime he delivered more than forty thousand sermons, seldom less than three a day. And the people listened to him. Sometimes his congregations reached twenty and thirty thousand.

As always when new things come along, there was opposition. It ranged all the way from bitter attacks in print by the clergy and "best" people to destructive riots. The day-by-day account of Wesley's activities in his *Journals* mentions more than sixty occasions when his meetings were disturbed by mobs. He was beaten, stoned, rolled in the mud, manhandled, and even threatened with death.

There was something persuasive and attractive about this courageous man with the fervent voice and quiet, searching face. Wherever he went he won men to his cause. The leader of one vicious mob suddenly said, "Sir, I will spend my life for you: follow me, and not one soul here shall touch a hair of your head." He became a leader in the Methodist cause. When Wesley was getting a shave, his barber said, "Sir, I praise God on your behalf. When you were at Bolton last, I was one of the most eminent drunkards in all the town; but I came to listen at the window, and God struck me to the heart. He gave me faith, and his love has ever since filled my heart." It was like that everywhere. Rough, uneducated people, whose religion had been dead and meaningless, were "born again," and became decent, God-fearing Christians. The outbursts of emotion which sometimes accompanied these conversions seemed to Wesley a special evidence that God's spirit was in their midst. To those who followed Wesley there was no doubt that their fervent faith was the sign of true religion.

50. Methodists

Wesley knew that men would need help if they were to live changed lives. It is no easy matter suddenly to stop drinking or swearing or stealing. So the Methodist Societies were organized everywhere in order that the members could seek "the power of godliness" and "watch over one another in love." The societies would have regular services with prayer, hymn-singing, and preaching. In addition, however, each member belonged to a band or class of eight or ten. These groups met each week to give one another advice and discipline.

Wesley had not wanted to separate from the Church of England but only to revive it. From the beginning he had been helped by a few other ministers—especially his brother Charles, a gifted hymn-writer, and George Whitefield, a most powerful preacher. And soon there were not enough preachers to satisfy the growing societies. Then some of his lay-leaders began to preach—men like Thomas Maxfield, a stone mason, and John Nelson and Thomas Olivers. Wesley was at first inclined to stop them but changed his mind when he saw their power and earnest spirit. Since the bishops refused, Wesley ordained men to serve as ministers in the chapels. He sent some of these preachers to America where they established churches throughout the colonies. Gradually after Wesley's death, the Methodists, with their societies, chapels, preachers, and thorough organization became entirely separate from the Church of England.

The Methodists were not plaster saints. They had their troubles. John Wesley himself with his dictatorial ways must have been hard to get along with at times. Nevertheless the Methodist movement changed England. Wesley himself lived to see some of this . "Falmouth," he noted, "is not now what it was ten years ago. All is quiet from one end to the other."

Wesley's Christianity, however, did not stop with an "inward kingdom." He attacked slavery, the liquor traffic, smuggling, wastefulness and greed in the use of money, cruel penal laws, corrupt elections, war, class pride, sweatshop labor, the kidnapping of men for naval service. He advocated, on the other hand, prison reform, public education, morality in government, land division, just wages. He put out popular editions of great books for the reading of the uneducated. For the poor he set up lending and relief organizations and a free medical service. At one point he arranged a simple industry to provide work for the unemployed.

Wesley's combination of practical Christianity, upright living, and spiritual faith influenced all the churches. His spirit entered deeply into the consciousness of English society and laid the foundation for the amazing reforms in the next century.

XI

To America

51. Beginnings

Protestantism came to America from England. In the seventeenth century there appeared along the Atlantic seaboard a series of settlements mainly of English origin although the French had founded Quebec in 1605. Most of the colonists came seeking a better living than crowded, land-hungry Europe had afforded. But some of the colonies were founded by deeply religious men seeking religious liberty. And many who followed them in the colonies were Protestant religious refugees.

Virginia was settled in 1607 though the poorly equipped adventurers almost perished. The Pilgrim Fathers came to New England's "stern and rock-bound coast" in 1620. Then in 1628 a "great migration" brought thousands of Puritans to Massachusetts. In wave after wave people came until by the end of the century there were settlements all along the coast. In addition to Englishmen Scotch-Irish followed from northern Ireland, Salzburgers from Austria, Germans from the Palatinate, and Huguenots from France.

Among them were to be found all varieties of Protestantism —many which we have not even been able to mention. As fierce persecution created trouble for one group and another now here and now there, the sturdier often found a way to get to America. The majority of those who came to the new land seeking economic opportunity happened to be Protestants.

Church of England (Episcopalians) came first. The settlers at Jamestown (1607) had a chaplain with them who conducted their first communion service in the new world under an old sail hung from some trees. The Episcopal Church was established officially in Virginia, and then later on in Maryand, New York (after it was taken from the Dutch), the Carolinas, and Georgia. Although the church had the protection of the royal governors, it usually was a minority church without much popular support.

Most of the Puritans who came to New England believed in

the Established Church but wanted to purify it. In Massachusetts and later in other colonies they had their chance. They set up an official church supported by taxes but without bishops. The church government which they finally worked out after a generation or two was Congregationalist.

Baptists were to be found throughout the colonies but for a time they centered in Rhode Island whose founder, Roger Williams, made it "a shelter for persons distressed for conscience." In accordance with Anabaptist principles church and state were separated and every man protected in the "peaceful and quiet enjoyment of lawful right and liberty."

Presbyterians were mainly Scotch refugees from Church of England persecution in north Ireland. They were rough and aggressive settlers who often simply took over unoccupied land and insisted that it is "against the laws of God and nature" to leave it idle when people need it to raise their bread. They spread throughout the colonies but were particularly strong in New York, New Jersey, and Pennsylvania.

The greatest variety of churches was to be found in the middle colonies—and nowhere more than in Pennsylvania. Penn's principles of complete liberty of conscience and separation of church and state were widely advertised and wonderfully attractive not only to Quakers but to continental refugees as well. When the American Revolution began, Pennsylvania had 403 different congregations—German Reformed, Presbyterian, Lutheran, Quaker, Episcopalian, Baptist, Moravian, Mennonite, Brethren, Catholic, and Dutch Reformed.

The first Lutherans came to America among the Dutch settlers of New York in 1623 and 1625. Others founded the Swedish colony of Delaware in 1638. The largest number came later, however, from Austria and Germany. They settled first in Georgia and Pennsylvania and then spread into Maryland and Virginia. Some leaders rapidly adopted English speech and ways but many remained isolated for several generations.

52. The Great Awakening

Not more than a small portion of the settlers in any of the colonies belonged to any of these churches. It took time for people who had been used to almost automatic church membership to adjust to a situation where they had to seek it deliberately. Many of the immigrants were drawn from the lower groups in society where the churches had almost lost their hold in England. Many, like the German Lutherans, who came seeking an opportunity to earn a better living, were without pastors and spiritual leadership. In the isolated and widely scattered communities of the new world they were often without regular worship for years.

Religious leaders throughout the colonies were aware of the declining spiritual condition. The fervor of the fathers had disappeared among the children. All this was changed by the "Great Awakening." The movement began among the Dutch Reformed in New Jersey, but its most famous leader was the brilliant New England pastor **Jonathan Edwards**. Wherever the revival went, people flocked to the services and began to think seriously about their sins. There was emotional excitement. Strong men fell over; women became hysterical; people wept and groaned.

Like a great tidal wave this emotional, religious revival swept through the communities and churches of America.

Thousands of unchurched people were, as one pastor put it, "effectually and lastingly changed into pious, uniform Christians." In one section of Virginia, for example, membership jumped from 291 in 1774 to 4,379 in 1777. In New England many parishes grew mightily and one hundred and fifty new Congregational churches were formed between 1740 and 1760.

Most important of all the revival movement marked the beginning of what became the great Protestant churches of America. Presbyterians, Baptists, and Methodists made a clear bid to reach people everywhere. Here was a technique which was to be used again and again on the frontiers.

It is clear that Protestant Christianity in America was different from anything in Europe. For one thing it was dominated by radical churches which in Europe had almost never had a chance. English Dissenters, Quakers, Baptists, Mennonites, Moravians, Methodists, all of them had been repressed and persecuted at one time or another. Even majority churches like the Lutheran were represented in America by their most zealous and pious members.

Moreover in America all the churches were faced with variety. No church was in a position to lord it over all the others. There were some difficult times, but Christians just had to learn to get along with each other. This made toleration and Christian brotherhood absolutely essential. Dreams of personal freedom and church life separated from state control suddenly blossomed and became real.

Americans discovered that freedom had its price. If members were to manage their own religious affairs without interference by the government, they could not expect the state to pay the bill. So they had to learn to support their churches by voluntary contributions. This was a difficult lesson every generation of immigrants had to learn.

53. Foundations of Liberty

It should not be supposed that the fortunate condition of liberty in the colonies was easily achieved. We are so accustomed to it in the United States and Canada today that we take it for granted as though it just naturally happened. The story so far should make it clear that many who came to these shores would have been quite happy to transplant European patterns of state control. This was in fact the situation that prevailed in both Virginia and New England. In Quebec the Catholics held the upper hand. Yet religious liberty came. There were many reasons.

Many of the colonies were started as business enterprises. Their success depended on settlers. Even when owners had no such deep convictions as motivated William Penn, they were nevertheless inclined to adopt a liberal policy in order to attract colonists. Maryland's Toleration Act of 1649 was pushed through the Provincial Assembly by "the lash of the Proprietor's whip" and against considerable opposition.

Church membership was proportionately small. Colonists escaping compulsory church connections often did not bother or were not able to join churches in America. Probably more than ninety per cent of the people were outside any church. Naturally they could not be expected to give much support to the idea of a state church.

Of utmost importance was the persistent agitation of dissenting church groups—Quakers, Baptists, Presbyterians. All had had experience with persecution. The Baptists, especially, prompted by clear-cut conviction, fought in season and out for an end to religious favoritism by government. A single national religion in either the United States or Canada became more than ever an impossibility.

By the time of the American Revolution the colonies had had considerable experience both with and without established churches. The dissatisfaction of minority groups without liberty and the striking success of colonies where liberty was granted helped pave the way for the policy of freedom.

In the United States the hard, practical realities of the religious situation were most important of all. The largest body was probably the Congregational church but even it did not have more than twenty per cent of the churches. How could Congregationalists, Presbyterians, Baptists, Episcopalians, Mennonites, Quakers, Reformed, Catholics, Jews, Methodists, and Lutherans get along together under one Federal govern-

129

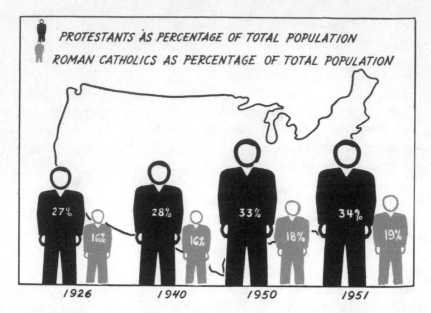

PROTESTANTS AS PERCENTAGE OF TOTAL POPULATION

ROMAN CATHOLICS AS PERCENTAGE OF TOTAL POPULATION

27%   16%   28%   16%   33%   18%   34%   19%

1926   1940   1950   1951

ment? There was just one answer—by separating church affairs completely from government and giving complete religious freedom to all but preferred status to none.

54. Makers of Liberty

Most of all religious liberty was the work of people—of individuals and obscure groups who toiled and thought and suffered to see that a principle was enshrined in the very life of a new nation.

Roger Williams was banished from Massachusetts for his views and had to flee in the dead of winter. He founded Rhode Island on the principle of complete religious freedom and absolute separation of government from the management of spiritual matters.

Obadiah Holmes was arrested in Massachusetts for his Baptist convictions and preaching. He was sentenced to be fined or "well whipped." He refused to allow friends to pay the fine. When his cruel punishment was ended, he said to the magistrate, "You have struck me as with roses."

William Robinson, Marmaduke Stevenson, and Mary Dyer, Quakers, deliberately went to Boston, as they put it, "to bear testimony against the persecuting spirit." They were hanged. Mary Dyer was offered freedom if she would simply leave but she replied, "Nay, I cannot." A spectator who saw her lifeless body swinging in the wind joked, "She hangs there as a flag." She was indeed—a symbol of loyalty, God's voice in her soul.

William Penn said: "I abhor two principles in religion and pity them that own them: the first is obedience to authority without conviction; and the other is destroying them that differ from me for God's sake." He suited action to conviction and established a colony with a liberal charter which granted freedom of worship to all who believed in "One Almighty God." The wonderful success of Penn's colony helped prove that a state could exist in which many churches were freely permitted.

George Mason, an Episcopalian vestryman, wrote the first draft of a Declaration of Rights for Virginia. Thomas Jefferson used it in the Declaration of Independence, and later it became the basis of the Bill of Rights in the Constitution of the United States. It opposed "force or violence" in religious matters and declared that "all men are equally entitled to the free exercise of religion, according to the dictates of conscience."

Samuel Livermore, an Episcopalian judge from New Hampshire, was a member of Congress when the Bill of Rights amendments were under debate. James Madison proposed one to read that "no national religion shall be established by law." Livermore was not satisfied with this and moved a more inclusive wording—"that Congress shall make no laws touching religion, or infringing the rights of conscience." Madison withdrew his motion and Livermore's was adopted—the First Amendment to the United States Constitution.

John Carroll, the first Roman Catholic bishop in the United States, delayed his consecration a year in order to have the traditional medieval phrase "exterminate heretics" omitted from the list of his duties.

Thomas Jefferson was the author of the Virginia "Bill for Establishing Religious Freedom." Finally enacted in 1785 it provided "that no man shall be compelled to frequent or sup-

port any religious worship," but that "all men shall be free to profess" and maintain any religious opinions they wish without effect on their civil rights. This is thought to be the first time in history that a state arranged for religious freedom and equality by its own choice.

And there were many others too: George Washington and Patrick Henry, John Leland, and the unnamed Baptists of Virginia who studied and agitated and addressed respectful petitions to the Assembly until freedom was won, and the Scotch-Irish Presbyterians who knew too much about religious oppression to forget. Together, named and unnamed, remembered and unremembered, they helped to forge a wonderful heritage which others have imitated.

The principle thus worked out in several colonies, developed by many advocates, expressed in the Virginia Bill and finally enshrined in the United States Constitution was not adopted automatically by the states. It took a generation for some to catch up. Not until 1833 did Massachusetts give up its state-supported Congregational Church. Slowly state constitutions were modified to bring them into accord with prevailing United States practice.

55. Making Freedom Work

The task in the United States during these hundred and sixty years has been to make what was imbedded in law work in practice. There have been problems. Americans have not always remembered the meaning of their laws. Occasional outbursts of religious prejudice and intolerance have marred community life. There are traditions that people with church connections cannot be elected to certain offices. The Know-Nothings and the Nativists, the American Protective Association and the Ku Klux Klan in different generations expressed an ugly bigotry against Roman Catholics. In Canada almost the opposite has been true where the Catholic majority in some provinces has shown bigotry towards the Protestants.

Moreover it has taken time to work out the exact implications of the principles. Church and State are separate but in America they are not—as in many modern European countries—hostile to each other. What relationships, then, are proper? Should clergymen be permitted to hold public office? Should the state enact laws to maintain the observance of Sunday? What support can the state give to church-controlled institutions — schools, hospitals, homes and the like? Can public health laws against the use of common cups be applied to the celebration of the Lord's Supper with the common cup? How much religion can there be in public education? Can the Bible be read in public schools? Can Christmas carols be sung in them? Should Jehovah's Witnesses be compelled to salute the flag? Should parochial schools be supported out of public funds? Is it constitutional for the government to employ ministers as chaplains in legislative bodies, in the Army and Navy, in state and local institutions such as hospitals, prisons, and the like? Slowly these and other questions are being answered in such a way as to make possible sympathetic co-operation, complete separation, and the utmost in freedom.

56. Frontier Religion

Today America is a land of many churches. Scarcely a community scattered across the continent in the United States or Canada lacks a church of some kind. More than half of the peoplé maintain a sufficiently active connection with some religious body to be counted as members. Yet at the time of the Revolution membership was less than ten per cent. How was this stupendous growth accomplished?

In all their history American churches have faced no challenge greater than that of the frontier. In one hundred and sixty years the United States, for example, grew from a few million people to almost one hundred and sixty million and expanded from some sparsely settled communities on the Atlantic seaboard to a giant nation spanning the continent. From the older eastern communities streams of pioneers and settlers pushed through the Appalachians into the central plains. They occupied the west coast and invaded the Rockies until at last, about sixty years ago, there was no more frontier. And all the while floods of immigrants from every part of Europe helped to swell the tide.

The churches might easily have given up in dismay at the size of the task. Never had there been one like it. Instead they rose to the occasion. The great churches of America today are those which most vigorously met the challenge—Presbyterian, Baptist, Methodist, and, in a different way, Lutheran.

Techniques differed. The Presbyterians were conservative and somewhat less adaptable to new conditions. Only as new areas had sufficient members to support a pastor was one sent in. In keeping with their tradition, however, they were active in establishing educational institutions.

Baptists were closer to the westward movement for they were more strongly represented among the poor farmers and landless workers who responded to the lure of cheap land. Baptist preachers came from the people. They seldom had much formal education (book learning was not highly regarded) and were often self-supporting. Here was a flexible and informal system readily adapted to frontier conditions.

Even more successful were the Methodists. They put their preachers on horseback and called them "circuit-riders." They had no settled congregations but traveled over an assigned territory holding meetings and organizing "classes." It might take a preacher five weeks to cover a circuit. He was seldom particular about the place he preached—a log cabin, a tavern barroom, a grove of trees—and he never waited to find Methodists. He aimed to make Methodists and Christians out of the people he found.

Life in the frontier communities was rough, raw, and disorderly. The churches did not hesitate to speak out against drinking, fighting, gossiping, lying, stealing, immoral sex relations, gambling, and horse racing. Stern discipline was used against backsliding members. In many cases the church was for years the only institution standing for law and order.

Spiritual zeal was aroused from time to time by revivals. This was a typically American technique developed on the frontiers. It involved a high degree of emotional appeal designed to call men from their evil ways and made them practicing Christians and church members. Camp meetings were revivals carried on for several days so people would have to gather and stay in tents. Excited appeals made to throngs of people at night by the flickering light of camp fires often produced shrieks and sobs and sometimes "the jerks." The emotional side of these methods was sometimes harmful, but there is also no doubt that these methods transformed many frontier areas and brought thousands of people into the churches.

57. Discord

As the United States grew so, too, did the churches. Everywhere they founded schools and colleges to train leaders. The churches themselves began to create nation-wide organizations and agencies through which to do their work. Sunday schools, various types of home and foreign mission societies, publication houses were developed.

The restlessness of the 1830s and 40s was reflected in the churches. Controversies of all kinds led to splits. Anti-Catholic sentiment was strong and ugly. Strange new churches sprang up—usually in response to needs which the older bodies had ignored. The Mormons followed Joseph Smith, and under Brigham Young founded a religious community in Utah. Various Adventist groups laid great stress on the second coming of Jesus. William Miller and his followers expected the end of ·

the world somewhere between March 1843 and March 1844. Holiness churches (like the Pentecostal) stressed possession of "the spirit" and a very narrow type of personal morality. Faith healing groups tried to cure physical ailments without medical help. A number of communistic religious communities were established. Contention reached a climax over slavery. When the Civil War came, most American churches had already divided into northern and southern branches. Protestant churches especially in New England had played a leading part in creating the moral sentiment against Negro slavery.

58. Larger Growth

With the close of the Civil War the United States turned again to westward expansion. New waves of immigrants from Europe flooded into the country, sometimes as many as a million in a single year. The fact that so many of them were from Germany and the Scandinavian countries more than any other one thing helped to make the Lutheran Church a major denomination in America. But every church met these new opportunities with enthusiastic zeal. Robert Ingersoll, the famous atheist, made the statement one day in an address that "the churches were dying out all over the land." A Methodist mission secretary sent him word that they were building a new church for every day in the year and hoped "to make it two a day." Soon Methodists were singing enthusiastically:

> The infidels, a motley band,
>   In council met and said:
> "The churches die all through the land,
>   The last will soon be dead."
> When suddenly a message came,
>   It filled them with dismay:
> "All hail the power of Jesus' name!
>   We're building two a day."

Meanwhile the United States moved into the age of Big Business. Handsome and expensive churches appeared. Contributions increased. Organization became more complicated. Sunday schools became an established part of church life. More

and more missionaries were sent to preach the gospel in Asia and Africa.

Some Christians began to look more sharply at life about them and discovered a lot of things which seemed un-Christian —vast slums in the cities, child labor, terrible working conditions, long killing hours (until after World War I tens of thousands of workers in the steel industry worked twelve hours a day, seven days a week), starvation wages, the heavy toll of industrial accidents, race prejudice, alcoholism, corrupt politics, divorce, and war. Gradually the bitterness which divided rival churches declined and some people began to think of better ways to meet America's moral and spiritual problems.

As a result a whole series of co-operative Protestant agencies developed—the American Bible Society, the International Sunday School Association, the Young Men's Christian Association and the Young Women's Christian Association, the Women's Christian Temperance Union, the Christian Endeavor Society, many others. Eventually in 1908 the churches themselves formed the Federal Council of Churches of Christ in America. In 1950 these groups were re-organized to form the **National**

Council of the Churches of Christ in the United States of America. Its parallel in Canada is the Canadian Council of Churches. In 1948 most of the Protestant Christian churches of the United States and Canada joined with scores of similar churches in other nations to form the World Council of Churches. The National Council, the Canadian Council, and the World Council are not churches. They are channels through which various denominations can work together intelligently and effectively at common tasks.

More than ninety per cent of American Protestants belong to a few great churches each of which has thousands of congregations and millions of members. There is scarcely a community throughout the land where at least one is not represented. They maintain their distinctive forms of worship and belief and organization. Yet each has a common Protestant heritage. They agree on the great essentials of evangelical Christianity, such as the authority of the Bible and salvation through faith in Jesus Christ.

Today they are working together at a multitude of Christian tasks and bearing their common witness to the Christian faith. Nobody thinks seriously that they will soon cease to exist. But these churches are more disposed than ever before to face the great tasks of this day together. Together they are continuing the effort to win not only the people of the United States and Canada but also the world to faith in Jesus Christ.

59. Lutheran Beginnings

The story of the Lutheran Church in North America in many ways parallels the development of Protestantism as a whole. Yet there are some notable differences.

The first Lutherans to reach the colonies were Dutch. They settled in Albany, New York in 1623. Two years later others were among the founders of New Amsterdam (New York City). Swedish Lutherans were to be found in New Sweden (Delaware) and Austrian Lutherans settled in Georgia. The main strength of colonial Lutheranism, however, was to be found in William Penn's colony. Among the thousands of Germans who sought a refuge there from poverty and persecution were many Lutherans. Some of them managed to form congregations but most of them were so poor, so scattered, so disorganized, and so handicapped by the language barrier that little more than survival was accomplished.

The formation of an organized Lutheran Church in America was in large part the work of a young German pastor, **Henry Melchior Muhlenberg.** He arrived in Philadelphia in November, 1742, "a stranger" who "did not know which way to turn." He set about establishing himself at once among the Lutheran people who had been plagued and victimized by a variety of drunken school teachers, ex-druggists, and vagabonds who had passed themselves off as pastors and tried to take charge of the congregations for their own profit.

Muhlenberg was patient, tactful, well-educated, sincere. Soon he had won the loyalty of the people and plunged into a vigorous round of parish activities. Church buildings had to be erected. A simple thing like a chalice (cup) for communion was hard to get. The German settlers had little money and what they could spare Muhlenberg directed to building. "My clothes are still holding out, though subject to much wear" from travel, he wrote. Several times he had to borrow money to replace them. However, there was plenty to eat. "One man brings me a sausage; another a piece of meat, a third a chicken, a fourth a loaf of bread, a fifth some pigeons, a sixth rabbits, a seventh eggs."

Gradually the work developed. Muhlenberg realized almost at once that help was needed and sent urgent requests back to Europe. For himself he rode back and forth among his parishes at Providence, New Hannover, and Philadelphia in cold, snow, rain, and heat. Always he was preaching, teaching, confirming, baptizing, building. Soon calls came from more distant places. Muhlenberg was especially in demand as a settler of disputes. There were visits (sometimes several) to Raritan and Hackensack in New Jersey, to New York City, to Easton and York in Pennsylvania, to Frederick in Maryland. The winter of 1774 he spent in Georgia.

In 1748 a most significant step was taken. Six Lutheran ministers and twenty-four lay delegates representing ten congregations met in Philadelphia. A form of worship was adopted, St. Michael's Church was dedicated, and Nicholas Kurtz was ordained minister. Muhlenberg himself presided at the conference or synod which later became known as the Ministerium of Pennsylvania. This was the beginning of an over-all organization for the Lutherans of America.

When the American Revolution ended, there were dozens of strong Lutheran churches scattered through the colonies though chiefly in Pennsylvania. Everywhere there were Lutheran people among the immigrants who poured into the country and joined the westward movement of pioneers. Yet there were not nearly enough pastors to meet their spiritual needs, and reinforcements from Europe were woefully small in number. The language barrier was a troublesome issue in the church. Leadership and organization were needed if the Lutheran Church was to become a real part of life in the United States. Both needs were soon met.

During the years since Muhlenberg first presided over the organization of the Ministerium of Pennsylvania other Lutheran synods had been formed—in New York, North Carolina, Ohio, Maryland, Virginia, Tennessee, South Carolina, elsewhere to the west in Pennsylvania itself. The weakness of these scattered synods was evident, so in 1820 in Hagerstown, Maryland the "General Synod of the Lutheran Church in the United States" was organized. The aim of this federation was to help the participating synods work together in meeting their needs and above all to organize a theological seminary for the training of a native ministry. There were many difficulties at first but in 1826 a seminary was finally started at Gettysburg, Pennsylvania.

These steps were of the greatest importance. They meant that Lutherans had come to America to stay, that they would no longer be dependent on German support or guidance but were prepared to carry on as an independent, self-directing American Lutheran church.

60. United Lutheran Church

We have seen how other Protestant groups worked diligently to plant churches on the frontiers and preach the gospel. The

Lutheran church had a share in this task but in a somewhat different way. Throughout the nineteenth century waves of immigration brought German, Austrian, Danish, Swedish, Norwegian, and other north European settlers to the United States. In the twentieth century this tide of immigration swung to Canada. Many were Lutherans—or at least of Lutheran background. While many of the early immigrants were lost to other churches, millions were gathered into the various general Lutheran bodies which appeared. Many German Lutherans who stayed in the east became part of the General Synod. A band of conservative Saxon Lutherans formed the Missouri Synod in 1847. It grew rapidly especially in the central part of the nation. The various Scandinavian groups established their own synods and tried to win their countrymen who, especially after the Civil War, came in vast numbers.

Meanwhile growth brought its troubles to the General Synod. Many of the newcomers fresh from Germany had a sharp consciousness of their heritage as Lutherans. They were scandalized by what seemed the laxity and watered-down faith of some in the church who believed it desirable to adjust the Lutheran faith to the American scene. S. S. Schmucker, for example, who had been instrumental in organizing the General Synod, in his later years proposed to modify the Augsburg Confession. The storms of bitter argument and controversy, which led to the Civil War in the United States, raged through the Lutheran Church and led to the splitting off from the General Synod of the "General Council" including the Canada Synod (1867) and the "United Synod of the South" (1862).

For two generations General Synod and General Council went their separate and often hostile ways. Throughout the East and Midwest they carried on parallel and sometimes competing work. They established congregations in the growing frontier communities and in the expanding cities. They sent missionaries abroad to preach the gospel. They published papers, prepared Sunday school literature, and discussed theology with each other. They co-operated in preparing a new Lutheran liturgy and hymnal, the *Common Service Book*.

For all the strains and harsh personal feelings it soon became clear that the General Synod and General Council had much in common. More and more enterprises were undertaken together. The adoption of the new Common Service meant that most of them were worshiping in the same way. Even the doctrinal issue which had originally caused much of the trouble gradually disappeared. The General Synod definitely rejected the liberalism of its radical wing and moved steadily in a conservative direction until it stood in practically the same position as the General Council. By the time they had worked together during World War I and had celebrated the four hundredth anniversary of the Reformation in 1917 they were ready to unite. In November 1918, General Synod, General Council, and United Synod of the South formed the **United Lutheran Church in America.** The United Lutheran Church extended throughout the United States and Canada.

61. Other Lutherans

Meanwhile similar developments were taking place among Lutherans elsewhere in America. The **Missouri Synod** spread far beyond its original state and became a strong, nation-wide Lutheran Church but so exclusive that it has had few formal relationships with other churches in the United States and Canada. It is a vigorous body with large and varied enter-

LUTHERAN CHURCHES IN TH

	ULCA	Missouri	American	Augustana
Congregations	4,591	5,450	4,891	1,24{
Ministers	4,872	5,947	4,708	1,29{
Baptized Mem.	2,477,012	2,387,292	2,257,169	605,38(
Confirmed Mem.	1,676,053	1,518,394	1,480,086	406,37{
Sun. Sch. Pupils	883,270	771,452	730,792	200,60{
Council Mem.	N C	S	N C	N C
Backgrounds	18th Cent. German	19th Cent. German	German, Norwegian, Danish	Swedish

N–National Lutheran Council   C–Canadian L

prises, notably the biggest Protestant parochial school system.

Swedish Lutherans organized the **Augustana Synod** in 1870. Gradually it became a general body like others in America. A number of synods chiefly in the Midwest and of German background united in 1930 to form the **American Lutheran Church**. A series of mergers among Norwegian groups resulted finally in the **Norwegian (later Evangelical) Lutheran Church in America** (1917). So the process goes on. Among all these Lutheran groups there were no major differences. Their separate existence was more the result of differences in age, language, geography, and European background. As these differences disappeared, mergers took place.

The immediate result is the most important development in the recent history of the Lutheran Church in America—the formation and growth of the **National Lutheran Council**. The council was formed as a result of experience during World War I when the various groups had worked together for soldiers' and sailors' welfare. The Council is not a church but an agency of the churches to carry out tasks they give it. A similar body, the **Canadian Lutheran Council**, has been formed in Canada.

World War II brought an enormous expansion of the National Lutheran Council and its work. Because of Lutheran World Action American servicemen could stroll into Lutheran

UNITED STATES AND CANADA

Wisconsin	Lutheran Free	Suomi	American Evangelical	Others
833	343	154	79	369
844	254	103	81	315
374,433	83,596	36,264	23,952	68,750
231,356	54,804	24,564	16,198	44,995
54,072	31,492	12,841	5,388	22,148
S	N C	N	N	
19th Cent. German	Norwegian	Finnish	Danish	Mixed

*an Council   S—Synodical Conference

Service Centers in New York and Chungking, in Charleston and Manila, in San Francisco and Paris. Because of LWA stranded European Lutheran missionaries and missions in the Pacific Islands, India, and Africa were able to keep going. Because of LWA, rubble churches rose amid the ruins of German cities, pastors were given bicycles and books, vestments and vitamins; Christians were trained for work behind the Iron Curtain and equipped with Christian literature; Arab refugees living in tattered tents received that pitiful measure of clothing and food which at least makes life possible; and Protestant DPs from Europe's terror were helped to a new life.

Almost all the Lutheran churches in the United States and Canada have participated in the wide variety of Christian services in Lutheran World Action. More than $59,000,000 and 746 million pounds of food and clothing, were contributed since 1946 to strengthen "Love's Working Arm." And in many corners of the globe the name of Christ is blessed because Lutherans in the United States and Canada have worked together in this conspicuous evidence of their faith and expression of their love.

For more than a hundred years the Lutheran Church in America stuck strictly to its own affairs, minding its business and trying to win and organize the multitudes who flocked to the United States and Canada from Europe. Today Lutherans have become one of the three largest Protestant groups. Moreover the day of isolation is dead. They are learning not simply to exist but to lift their voices in the councils of the churches. They are reaching out to join with fellow Christians both in the **Lutheran World Federation** and in the World Council of Churches. American Lutherans have become a vigorous part of a moving enterprise, a mighty company, a major force in Protestant Christianity, witnesses to the faith.

From all these things we see the signs of further pages in a thrilling story which began when kings were bishops and bishops were kings. What would Martin Luther have thought if he could have seen the vast unfolding of that story he had begun almost without intention? Could he have dreamed what the end would be? Can we?

144

Information Please

Session 1

1. How many churches are there in your community?

2. Why do we have these various churches? How do they differ? In what ways are they similar? What do they stand for? What do they do in your community?

3. What can you say about each church (or church group) as to:

    a) Its worship?   c) Its organization?
    b) Its beliefs?   d) Its life?

4. If all churches were alike would there be any advantages? Any disadvantages?

5. When, where, and how did the Christian church begin?

Session 2 (Sections 1-4 of this book)

1. What were the results for the church of the favors which Constantine bestowed upon it?

2. Who was Hildebrand?

3. For what should each of these popes be remembered: Gregory VII, Innocent III, Boniface VIII?

4. Why did the popes at Rome feel they should rule over states as well as the church? What arguments did they use?

5. What was *excommunication?* What was the *interdict?*

6. What other illustrations do you find in pages 9 to 16 of the relationship of church and state?

Sessions 3 and 4 (Sections 5-7)

1. What was wrong with priests in the church before the Reformation? What were *pluralism* and *absenteeism?*

2. What did Christians in the Middle Ages believe about witches, saints, relics, and the Virgin Mary?

3. What were *indulgences?* What was the *treasury of merit?*

4. How did the popes like Julius II become so wealthy?

5. Is it true to say that medieval Christianity was more concerned with this world than the next?

6. What were the sacraments of the Roman Church?

Session 5 (Sections 8-10)

How would you identify each of the following:

1. John Huss
2. Savonarola
3. Inquisition
4. Erasmus
5. Peter Waldo

6. Humanists
7. Cathari
8. Mystics
9. John Wyclif
10. Heresy

Session 6 (Sections 11-12)

1. What were Martin Luther's parents like?
2. What kind of discipline did Luther receive at home? In school?
3. What subjects did Martin Luther study at school?
4. What was popular Christianity like? What was *purgatory?*
5. How did the church say a man could be saved?
6. Why did Luther become a monk?

Session 7 (Sections 13-17)

On a separate piece of paper mark True (T) or False (F) beside the number for each of the following statements.

1. A tonsure is part of a monk's clothing.
2. Monks promised always to remain obedient, poor, and unmarried.
3. Luther's personal religious revolution was the result of his study of the writings of the church fathers.
4. Luther's chief concern was to know how he stood before God.
5. Luther was afraid of God and at times even hated him.
6. Luther was never much troubled about the problem of sin.
7. Indulgences were issued by the church to reduce a man's time in purgatory.
8. According to Luther's doctrine of justification by faith men cannot win or earn God's favor.
9. Luther said men must win salvation by obeying exactly every command of God.

Session 8 (Sections 18-29)

1. What was *purgatory?*
2. What were *indulgences?* What was the common view of their significance?
3. What were Luther's Ninety-five Theses about?
4. Why did they stir up so much interest?
5. What happened at the Leipzig Debate?

146

Session 9 (Sections 21-22)

1. Mention one or two major ideas from each of these books by Martin Luther:

    a) On Good Works

    b) On the Papacy at Rome

    c) To the Christian Nobility

    d) On the Babylonian Captivity

    e) On Christian Liberty

2. What kind of a writer was Luther?

3. What was a *papal bull?*

4. Why did the little drama of December 10, 1520 make such an impression on people?

Session 10 (Sections 23-24)

1. Who were the following: Kaspar Sturm, Aleander, Charles V, Frederick, Huss?

2. What was the Church's argument against having Luther appear before the Diet at Worms?

3. Why did Luther go in spite of the danger?

4. What did Luther have to say before the Diet?

5. What did he appeal to as his religious authority?

6. What did the Diet decide to do about Luther?

Session 11 (Sections 25-27)

1. How did Luther feel about his "imprisonment" at the Wartburg?

2. What did he do while there?

3. What changes in church affairs took place at Wittenberg in Luther's absence?

4. What did Luther do about radicalism at Wittenberg?

5. Was Luther unsympathetic with the peasants? What criticisms did he make of them? Also of the nobles?

6. Identify each of the following: Knight George, Wartburg, Carlstadt, Bundschuh, Muntzer.

Session 12 (Sections 28-29)

1. Why did each of these groups stop following Luther: moderate Catholics? Scholars? Patriots? Peasants? Radicals?

2. In what ways did Protestant and Catholic disagree on the question of authority?

3. How did the Protestant approach to the Bible differ from that of the Roman Catholic?

4. When was Luther's German Bible published?

Session 13 (Section 30)

1. Why did Luther write his catechisms? What needs were they intended to meet?

2. What are the major sections of the *Small Catechism?*

3. How did Protestants get that name?

4. How did the Augsburg Confession come to be written?

5. What was its significance?

Session 14 (Section 31)

1. What difference is there in position between the Roman Catholic priest and the Protestant minister?

2. Why did Luther and his associates finally develop a new church organization? What was it like?

Sessions 15-16 (Section 32)

1. What was the *Mass* in the Roman Catholic Church?

2. What were the chief changes made by Luther in public worship?

3. How did Luther's conservative attitude differ from radical Protestants on the reformation of worship?

4. How would you describe Luther's preaching? Was preaching made more or less important by the Reformation?

5. What was the chief significance of music in the new Lutheran church? What was the music like?

Session 17 (Section 33)

1. Mention some of the typical features of Roman Catholic life in Luther's day.

2. What, according to Luther, is the motive for goodness? What should be its chief expression in our daily life?

3. Why did Protestants abolish the distinction between sacred and secular? Did they make everything sacred or everything secular?

4. Contrast Catholic and Protestant views on:

    a) Marriage and the home.

    b) Monastic life.

Session 18 (Sections 33-34)

1. Whom did Luther marry? When? Why?
2. What was Luther's family life like?
3. How many children were there in Luther's family? Where did the family live?
4. What kind of father was Martin Luther? How would you characterize his home?

Sessions 19-20 (Sections 35-36)

1. What do you feel were the most important features of Luther's character?
2. What was the Religious Peace of Augsburg?
3. How did the Reformation spread to Scandinavia?
4. What do you think were the greatest changes in the life of the average person resulting from the Reformation?

Sessions 21 and 22 (Sections 37-42)

1. Where did Zwingli do his work?
2. How did he differ from Martin Luther?
3. How did the Reformation develop in Switzerland?
4. What was John Calvin's ideal for Geneva? What was life like there under him?
5. Who was Servetus?
6. What were the distinctive features of Calvinism?
7. How did Calvin influence the French Reformation?
8. Who were the Huguenots? For what did they stand?
9. What was the Edict of Nantes?
10. Who were the "Sea Beggars"?
11. Who was William of Orange?
12. Who was John Knox?

Sessions 23, 24, and 25 (Sections 43-50)

1. Why did Henry VIII make himself head of the English Church?
2. Through what stages did the Reformation go under Edward VI, Mary, and Elizabeth?
3. Who were the Puritans? What did they stand for in religion? in politics?
4. Who were the rulers of England in the 17th century and what happened to the religious problem under each?
5. Who were the Separatists? Why were Christians persecuted in England especially under Charles II?

6. Who were the Congregationalists? For what did they stand?

7. Why were the Anabaptists persecuted? Where did the English Baptists come from?

8. What kind of man was John Wesley? What did he do for England?

9. Why were his followers called Methodists?

Session 26 (Sections 51-52)

1. What countries in Europe were the chief sources of American Protestantism?

2. What were the primary reasons for immigration to the English colonies?

3. Where particularly were the Episcopal, Baptist, Presbyterian, and Congregational churches to be found in the colonies?

4. Where were the most liberal religious policies in force in the colonies?

5. What was the *Great Awakening?* What was its effect?

Session 27 (Sections 53-55)

1. What were some of the chief reasons for the development of religious freedom in the American colonies? What contribution was made by the Baptists? By the Quakers?

2. What is the relationship today between church and government in the United States? In Canada?

Session 28 (Sections 56-58)

1. What was religious life like on the frontier? Compare the methods of expansion employed by the Baptists, the Presbyterians, the Methodists.

2. What were *revivals?*

3. What do you think was the most important achievement of the American churches in the 19th century?

Session 29 (Sections 59-61)

1. Where and when did Lutherans first settle in America?

2. Who was the first organizer of the Lutheran Church in America?

3. How did the United Lutheran Church come into being? What other major Lutheran bodies are there in the United States and Canada? Why are there so many?

4. What is the National Lutheran Council and what does it do? What is the Canadian Lutheran Council?

Difficult Words

Ascetic — denying oneself pleasures.

Bishop—the spiritual head and administrator of the churches of a district.

Bull—a papal letter.

Burgher—a freeman.

Canon—a rule or decree of the church.

Canton—a district in Switzerland similar to a small state.

Cardinal—a prince of the Roman Church, adviser to the pope. Cardinals elect the popes.

Cathedral — the church and headquarters of a bishop.

Chant — a type of singing where the same phrase or tone is very often repeated.

Cloister—see *Monk.*

College of Cardinals — the council of all Roman Catholic Cardinals.

Confession—see *Penance.*

Creed—a statement of what a person believes.

Crucifix — the cross with the figure of Jesus upon it.

Diet—a gathering of representatives of many German citics, states and principalities.

Dispensation — a release from a church law or obligation.

Ecclesiastical — related to the church.

Edict—a public notice or command.

Elector—a prince of the Holy Roman Empire entitled to help elect the Emperor.

Establishment, Established Church—an official church supported by the government.

Evangelical — having to do with the Gospel. See section 30.

Excommunicate—to prohibit a person from receiving the sacraments.

Gothic—the pointed-arch style of church architecture developed in medieval Europe and used for the great cathedrals.

Grace—the love and favor of God, his forgiveness.

Heritage—that which comes to one as his birthright.

Heretic—a person who rejects the church's teaching.

Idolatry—worshiping something other than God.

Indulgence—a pardon for sins secured through money payments which were substituted for the penalties the sins demanded. (See section 7, 18.)

Inquisition—a group of religious officials appointed to deal with heretics. (See section 8.)

Intercede—to act between two persons to settle differences.

Interdict—a law suspending religious ceremonies and sacraments in a city or a nation.

Layman—an ordinary church member, not a clergyman.

Justification—God's act of forgiveness through which sinners are treated as though they were righteous. (See section 16.)

Mass — the Lord's Supper of

151

the Roman Catholic Church. (See sections 7, 14, 32.)

Matins—a morning service of worship especially in a monastery.

Medieval—refers to the civilization which flourished in Europe from about 1000 to 1400; the Middle Ages.

Monastery — the home of monks.

Monasticism — the system of life which is followed by a monk.

Monk— an individual who goes apart from the world to live a life of religious devotion. Monks were bound to remain, poor, unmarried, and obedient. They belonged to *monastic* orders or societies and lived in monasteries or cloisters. Monks were called brothers. The women were called nuns or sisters. (See sections 12, 13.)

Novice—a candidate on trial for permanent admission to a monastic order.

Nun—see *Monk*.

Order—see *Monk*.

Penance — a Roman Catholic sacrament of forgiveness. It includes confession to the priest and the performance of satisfaction. (See section 7.)

Penitent—to be sorry for one's sins; to refer to the person who is sorry.

Piety—the quality of devotion and spirituality in an individual's daily life and conduct.

Prior—the head of a monastic house.

Public Disputation—a debate.

Purgatory — an intermediate

according to Roman Catholic theology, where a person atones for his sins. (See sections 12 and 18.)

Recant, recantation — to take back what has been declared.

Ritual — a religious ceremony or form of worship.

Sacraments — in the Roman Church the ceremonies in which God's grace is thought to come to the believer through the priest.

Scholastic—having to do with the philosophers and teachers (schoolmen) of the Middle Ages.

Secular — in or having to do with the world. The opposite of sacred. The word was used of a priest who ministered to a parish as distinguished from a "regular" who lived according to a rule in a monastery.

Serfdom — a system where a worker was practically a slave to the owner of the land on which he worked.

Theologian—a student of religion and the truths of God.

Theological — formal religious knowledge, study about God.

Temporal—having to do with this life.

Theocracy — a government where God is supposed to be the leader.

Tonsure—a special haircut for Monks. The hair was clipped high on the sides of the head and the crown shaved leaving a hairy circle.

Vestment — the special robes worn by ministers and priests when leading worship.

Vicar—a substitute priest.